JEET KUNE DO
WISDOM

José M. Fraguas

EMPIRE BOOKS/AWP LLC
Los Angeles, CA

DISCLAIMER: Please note that the author and publisher of this book are NOT RESPONSIBLE in any manner whatsoever for any injury that may result from practicing the techniques and/or following the instructions given within. Since the physical activities described herein may be too strenuous in nature for some readers to engage in safely, it is essential that a physician be consulted prior to training.

First Edition published in 2023 by AWP LLC/Empire Books.

EMPIRE BOOKS
P.O. Box 491788
Los Angeles, CA 90049

First edition. Library of Congress Catalog Number:
ISBN-13: **978-1-949753-63-9**

23 22 21 20 19 18 17 16 15 14 13 12

Library of Congress Cataloging-in-Publication Data:

Jeet Kune Do Wisdom / by Fraguas, Jose M.—1st ed. p. cm. Includes index.
ISBN 978-1-949753-63-9 (pbk.: alk. paper) 1. Jeet kune do. 5. Martial arts—technique. 3. Large type books. I. Title. GV1222.3.F715 20146069.715'3—dc24

2006012419

PRINTED IN THE UNITED STATES OF AMERICA

TABLE of CONTENTS

DEDICATION

To the memory of Brandon Lee, a good friend in search of his own path who made everyone around him better. His laughter will be forever missed.

ACKNOWLEDGEMENTS

I would like to thank all the instructors appearing in this book for supplying me not only with enormous amounts of their personal time for the long interviews but also with wonderful pictures from their personal archives to illustrate this work. Without their work ethic, sacrifice, and commitment to preserving Bruce Lee's legacy, there would not be a book.

My heartfelt thanks go to Linda Lee Cadwell and Shannon Lee for their support and trust throughout all these years. The importance of your contribution to preserving Bruce's legacy cannot be overstated.

Last, but not least, I offer my gratitude to Bruce Lee, who through his unwavering commitment to the truth made everything possible.

ABOUT THE AUTHOR

Born and raised in Madrid, Spain, Jose "Chema" Fraguas began his martial arts studies with judo, in grade school, at age 9. From there he moved to taekwondo and then to kenpo karate, earning a black belt in both styles. During this same period, he also studied shito-ryu karate and eventually received a seventh-degree black belt.

He began his career as a writer at age 16 by serving as a regular contributor to martial arts magazines in Great Britain, France, Spain, Italy, Germany, Portugal, Holland, and Australia. Having a black belt in three different styles allows him to better reflect the physical side of the martial arts in his writing. "Feeling before writing," Fraguas says.

In 1980, he moved to Los Angeles and was accepted as a student by Dan Inosanto at the Kali Academy. In his first struggling years he managed to meet numerous martial arts greats such as Gene LeBell, Hawkins Cheung, Jun Chong, Wally Jay, et cetera. He trained at the legendary

Main Street Boxing Gym in downtown L.A. in order to learn the "boxing hands" recommended by Dan Inosanto. The open-minded mentality taught at the Kali Academy helped him to develop an eclectic approach to the martial arts. Seeking to supplement and expand his personal training, he researched other disciplines such as wing chun, savate, muay Thai, wrestling, and jiu-jitsu.

In 1986, Fraguas founded his own book and magazine company in Europe, authoring dozens of books and distributing his magazines to 35 countries in three different languages. His reputation and credibility as a martial artist and publisher became well known to the top masters around the world.

Considering himself a martial artist first and a writer and publisher second, Fraguas feels fortunate to have had the opportunity to interview many legendary martial arts teachers. He recognizes that much of the information given in the interviews helped him to discover new dimensions in the martial arts.

"I was constantly absorbing knowledge from the great masters," he recalls. "I only trained with a few of them, but intellectually and spiritually all of them have made very important contributions to my growth as a complete martial artist."

Steeped in tradition yet looking to the future, Fraguas understands and appreciates martial arts history and philosophy and feels this rich heritage is a necessary steppingstone to personal growth and spiritual evolution. His desire to promote both ancient philosophy and modern thinking provided the motivation for writing this book.

"If the motivation is just money, a book cannot be of good quality," Fraguas says. "If the book is written to just make people happy, it cannot be deep. I want to write books so I can learn as well as share."

The author currently lives in Los Angeles.

FOREWORD

As early as I can remember, my house was filled with books. Many of these books—some new, some old—were excellent collections of quotations. My father and mother clipped quotes from magazines or newspapers, and even wrote some themselves and posted them on kitchen cabinets, the refrigerator and other special places for the family to see.

There are many pleasures to be derived from a book on quotations. There is the relief of finding something that has been buzzing in our minds, there is also the pleasure of finding some thought of which we approve but which we have not managed to express clearly and there is a purely retrospective delight. Of course, wisdom is meaningless until our own experience has given it meaning.

Through my childhood, reading and rereading these quotes has helped me to replace negatives thoughts with strong and positive alternatives. While words are not substitutes for the difficult physical and mental training required to master the martial arts, they are a relevant aspect of the transmission and the learning process of every student. *Jeet Kune Do Wisdom* is an anthology of the

best words said by the great teachers of the art developed by Bruce Lee. It examines different elements of the art, including its tradition, philosophy, general training, self-defense, et cetera.

All the instructors have expressed similar ideas in very different ways. Regardless of the words they used, there must be truth in the Jeet Kune Do philosophies and principles that so many different people have believed in

and lived by. The more I researched, the more I realized that those great teachers are more like you and me than they are different. They had difficult days and seemingly impossible hurdles, yet they endured and prevailed.

I have made every effort to present each quotation within its context as accurately as possible. In philosophical matters, it is syntax, more than vocabular, that needs to be corrected. Due to the limitations of language and linguistic expression when dealing with philosophical and spiritual matters, it is easy to understand why some of the ideas and principles of these masters are so complex, subtle and intricate—particularly if the ideas are studied out of context. If you try to apply some of these idea, don't forget that it is easier to quote somebody else than it is to really understand what they meant by saying it. There are obvious dangers in using words without being sure what we really mean. But there is another less obvious danger in trying to provide exact definitions—the danger is that we may think we have succeeded. As the philosopher Bertrand Russell wrote: "There is no more reason why a person who uses a word correctly should be able to tell what it means than there is why a planet which is moving correctly should know Kepler's laws." I respectfully would like to advise the reader to *listen* not to the words of the masters but to *what* they really meant when they said those words. The way of the martial arts produces a practitioner torn between the art and the mystic. The way of the artist and the way of the mystic are similar, but the mystic lacks a craft ... the physical techniques. The craft (physical training) keeps the artist in touch with the remarkableness of the world and in relationship to it. Therefore, philosophy without hard physical training is useless.

This book originated more than 12 years ago as a personal manuscript of life-affirming quotations for my own personal use. As I had the great opportunity to keep interviewing many of the greatest JKD Instructors in the world, the pages of the manuscript kept increasing until one day my mother asked me: "What are you planning to do with all these quotations?" As soon as I answered, "I don't know," she was pointing with her finger to the shelves of one of the bookcases at home where the complete collection of books on quotations was. She simply smiled and left the room.

Meeting the masters and having long conversations with them allowed me to do more than simply scratch the surface of the technical aspects of the art of Jeet Kune Do. It also helped me to research and analyze the human beings behind the teachers.

Years before anyone ever heard of any of them, they devoted themselves to their arts, often in solitude, sometimes to the exclusion of other pursuits most of us take for granted. They worked themselves into extra-ordinary physical condition and stayed there. They ignored distractions and diversions and brought to their training a great deal of concentration. The best of them got as good as they could possibly get at performing and teaching their chosen art, and the rest of us watched them and, leading our balanced lives, wondered how good we might have gotten at something had we devoted ourselves to whatever we did as ferociously as these masters embraced their arts. In that respect, they bear our dreams.

Most of what passed as human wisdom is merely the post-examination gabble of excited individuals trying to guess how the new lessons will explain the old questions of life and martial arts training. Anything is fresh on the first hearing…even though others may have heard it a thousand times through a score of generations.

In the spring of 2019, I finished the first draft of this work, took the manuscript and sent it to several JKD teachers. It was exciting to hear their comments. Many of them wrote kind words that they wanted me to use to support the project. Unfortunately, some of them won't see the final printed work, because they shed their mortal skin and returned to the sacred battlefields where the true warriors fight their battles. Their words are in this book because without them this work would never be completed.

More than three decades after my mother pointed to that old bookcase, here is the final work. Books are an essential part of my life and they have opened new and exciting avenues of life. My goal is to share these JKD thoughts with as many people as possible. I hope this collection provides comfort and inspiration for all JKD practitioners and martial artists—regardless of style—and for the casual browser and reader. If you, the reader, find this work useful as both a guide and a reference work and discover some unexpected sayings, the book will have served its purpose.

Enjoy.

José M. Fraguas

INTRODUCTION

By

José M. Fraguas

I moved to Los Angeles in 1980, where I was accepted as a student of Jeet Kune Do instructor Dan Inosanto, at the old Kali Academy in Torrance, California. It was a time when there was no confusion about the art. The terms "original JKD" or "JKD concepts" had not been coined yet and the turmoil and politics the art has experienced didn't exist. JKD was the art and the philosophy of Bruce Lee and the technical foundation was there to be learned. Any kind of training in another system was a supplementary training for personal growth or for developing specific attributes, and it was not JKD.

I never saw any contradiction in preserving the Lee material handed down to Dan Inosanto, Dan Lee, Ted Wong, Jerry Poteet, Bob Bremer, and the other first generation students and applying the JKD philosophy to "accommodate" and "assimilate" useful elements discovered through an intense and demanding personal learning process. I believe that once you start to transcend from the idea of "fighting" as your main focal point and reason for your martial arts training, your understanding of the art suddenly expands and reaches another level. You do your best to prepare yourself to fight and defend your life if you have to, but fighting is not really an issue anymore. You've already been through the process of "finding what is useful for combat" and developed that JKD "inquiring mind" and "functional eye." By having that knowledge, you don't become "caught" in that constant necessity of proving to your ego that you can beat the hell out of somebody else—which in the long run is just a psychological prison which prevents you from discovering a higher existence.

The philosopher said, "When the ego is dissolved there is no need to impress your fellowman." It's not a matter of dissolving the ego, because the ego cannot be dissolved; rather it is dealing with it according to the internalization of your own inner peace. Nevertheless, the understanding of the JKD art grows in the same manner that you grow as a person-through the process of being open-minded and receptive to everything around you. I've been very fortunate to have a job related to martial arts that does

not depend on teaching martial arts to make a living. I perceived that the art was not meant for mass distribution, but that it was dependent on its precepts being passed down in a very personal way.

That's why I decided, after returning to Europe in 1986, to keep a low profile, restricting my teaching to a very small group of "die hards" in a basement. Studying and training as much as I could, I concurrently analyzed the philosophies of Taoism, Zen, and Jiddu Krishnamurti to better understand the philosophy, conceptual structure, and roots of the JKD art. "If you understand the roots, you'll know the blossoms," the founder said. I have to gratefully acknowledge how valuable other JKD instructors

have been in helping me to understand my way to Jeet Kune Do. I feel truly grateful to all who contributed to my understanding of the art developed by Bruce Lee and pointed me in the right direction to find the truth as it applied to me.

In 1980, I was fortunate to be a small part of the historical Kali Academy, where Bruce Lee's presence hung in the air like autumn morning mist. If you didn't actually feel his being, you could always look at any wall which were adorned with his pictures, sayings, and teachings. When Dan Inosanto was teaching and the classes were underway, you got the strange feeling that Bruce Lee was looking over the proceedings. Only 17 years old, and feeling that I was living in a dream, I could barely talk to my JKD si-hings. Despite my awkwardness, they were kind enough to help me in every aspect that I needed, never refusing to correct a physical technique, clarify a philosophical principle, or grant an embarrassed request to borrow a sleeping bag.

I'm very grateful to my seniors who kindly shared the JKD oral traditions with me, allowing me to be a listener in their JKD inner-circle conversations. As much as anything, this helped me to develop myself both as a martial artist and a JKD practitioner. I feel sad for the discrepancies that I have seen grow among the members of the JKD family. I'm a firm believer that even "being a free and creative martial artist" does not excuse you from maintaining some important traditions in order to keep your own roots. The student's behavior will directly affect his instructor's reputation. The student's wrong acts and attitude "will heap fiery coals upon his sifu's head." Everyone should know what his position in the JKD family is and should act toward his elders, seniors, and instructors in a very respectful way. Bruce Lee firmly required the traditional address of "sifu" from his students—demanding it from Inosanto to Taky Kimura, and then from the students at the Chinatown kwoon to Dan Inosanto. Bruce Lee's modern approach to the technical aspects was not in opposition to his appreciation and respect for martial arts' deep traditional values.

Many of Bruce Lee's teachings dealt with individual philosophical development. A philosophy which is to have any value should be built upon a wide and firm foundation of knowledge which is not specifically "philosophical." Lee's philosophy was a battleground on which he fought a battle against himself; sometimes going one way and sometimes another. He covered the whole martial arts field before reaching conclusions diametrically opposed to those which he had followed in the earlier years of his martial career. The key to understanding Bruce Lee's philosophy is that it was essentially a by-product of his quest for knowledge. To treat it as though it were an end in itself is liable to render it meaningless.

A sculptor is symbolically described as a man who gets rid of unnecessary chips of marble; it is the same process known to every writer who whittles away unnecessary words from his manuscript, and to every mathematician and scientist who uses Occam's Razor to search for the most elegant proofs and theorems. It is the same method that Bruce Lee used for "shedding away the unessential for JKD techniques." Due to the limitations of language and

linguistic expression when dealing with philosophical and spiritual matters, it is easier to understand why Lee's writings were so complex, subtle and intricate—particularly if his ideas are studied out of context.

It's paramount to understand Bruce Lee's way of "doing" philosophy and what his roots were. It's easy to quote somebody else in order to justify our preferences and personal inclinations. However, there are obvious dangers in using words without being sure what we really mean by them. But there is another less obvious danger in trying to provide exact definitions—the danger is that we may think we have succeeded.

The great mathematician Lindemann showed that it is impossible to square the circle. Perhaps, and not only using an acute and original approach but also a self-critical one, we may be able to square our circle... "with no circumference."

HISTORY

The first "Tao of JKD" book is the closest to what he was sharing with us at the club. I remember what he said to me over the years was in that book.

Leo T. Fong

Bruce Lee probably only learned the *sizi nim tao* and *chum kiu* forms (two of the three empty-hand sets), part of the wooden dummy set, and never formally learned the two weapons of wing chun—the long pole and the double knives. Despite these limitations, however, Lee did have a profound connection to the art of wing chun.

Robert Chu

According to his personal records I had over 122 privates, but I can't remember the exact number. We used to meet Wednesday night, Saturday afternoon, and Sunday morning.

Ted Wong

When you are training a fighter to compete against another highly skilled athlete, there is no time for foolishness. Everything must be highly efficient, pressure tested, and modified for the individual fighter. This is exactly the mindset that Bruce Lee had in his JKD training; he just directed all of his energies toward preparing for a street altercation with no rules at all.

Burt Richardson

At the end of the class at Dan's, we'd spend maybe a half-hour working on the Filipino martial arts. Some of the guys stayed and some didn't. Basically, it was up to you. I really enjoyed the stick work, so I stayed most of the time.

Chris Kent

Jeet Kune Do in 1970 was a system that had been developed a few years ago with just a bunch of students practicing. No seminars, no videotapes, no hundreds of instructors around the world—just Dan Inosanto in Los Angeles, period.

Tim Tackett

When we are creating our own style, it is an investigation into what is the best way to get more power, more speed, more illusiveness for ourselves as individuals.

Cass Magda

I may be wrong, but didn't a certain "Little Dragon" once say, "Jeet kune do is only a name...please don't fuss over it"?

John Steven Soet

At the old Kali Academy, when a formal jeet kune do class still existed, you had your "technicians," your "hobbyists," your "movie stars in waiting," your "classroom warriors," your "asters(?!)," etc. Then you had a few people who actually listened to what Dan was trying to convey to us. These people were the *fighters*.

Paul Vunak

I had a magic three years with a genius and when he left that magic went away too. It was an admission that was very hard for me to make to myself.

Stirling Silliphant

The goal of martial arts is to avoid a fight. The reason most men fight is because they feel they have something to prove. The real martial artist has nothing to prove, therefore he has no need to fight.

Joe Hyams

For years I used to try to avoid politics with regards to JKD. But politics are a part of JKD just like they're a part of life. So I changed my perspective. Politics are about mutual accommodation, compromise, and understanding.

Chris Kent

Bruce was very straightforward. He would speak his mind right away and that offended some people when he criticized the technical structures of other styles. I am not that way.

Dan Inosanto

I remember Ted Wong commenting to me that the standard of sparring that he saw at my school in the senior class was higher than that of Chinatown. I think that in 20 more years the standard of JKD people will be even higher.

Cass Magda

One time while working at his house in Culver City, I walked into the kitchen. Bruce was at the kitchen counter. He shoved a paper in front of me and said, "This is for you" He said, "I don't give those out too often, and I think you should be proud of it." That piece of paper was my certificate.

Ted Wong

Lee also had the opportunity to learn from his seniors, the late Wong Shun Leung and William Cheung. Later, in Seattle, Lee had a chance to see wing chun from a different perspective thanks to Yeung Fook, a friend of his father from the opera, who practiced the Gulao system.

Robert Chu

Martial arts teach you discipline both mentally and physically. It takes a certain amount of discipline to push your body to operate in a specific, unusual, and well-coordinated way.

Taky Kimura

I have also been integrating the hard and soft energy in my JKD techniques in order to make them flow like water.

Dan Lee

I remember Dan Inosanto telling us that going to your teacher and learning a technique is like going to a man every day for a fish. You become dependent on the man who gives you the fish.

Tim Tackett

I'd like to preserve the art as Bruce Lee taught it to me. I was fortunate that Bruce Lee shared with me the material that he was working on and researching, and I want to preserve it to prevent it from completely disappearing.

Ted Wong

Bruce himself resisted making JKD a full-fledged commercial organization, even when he needed the money.

Jerry Poteet

Don't look for the answers in an authority figure or teacher. You have to take that inward journey to self-realization and liberation.

Ted Lucaylucay

The parties who feel that jeet kune do is an ongoing process and the parties who feel that Bruce Lee spent his life refining a devastating system, and that it would be like trying to reinvent the wheel to waste time dabbling in other areas, are both right.

John Steven Soet

The JKD people then didn't compete because we were already doing full contact sparring during the point tournament era. For us, it was going backwards.

Richard Bustillo

When I started at the Kali Academy in 1980, we learned fundamentals for two months and then were instructed to buy boxing gloves and a mouthpiece for the following week. That's when we started sparring. Unfortunately, that first night was quite wild and we lost a lot of students from the class after that first night of sparring. It was a good lesson for everyone.

Burt Richardson

It was a real shock when Bruce died. I still love him and miss him very much and I try to follow his teachings.

Larry Hartsell

Jerry Poteet called me one day and told me that Bruce was going to give a two-hour demonstration at the opening of his L.A. Chinatown school. I guess it was around the beginning of 1967.

Bob Bremer

The problem with the art of Jeet Kune Do is a direct result of our organization's connection with Bruce Lee, and the money-making potential some feel that a sanction from such an organization can generate.

Paul Vunak

So when Bruce left Hollywood for Hong Kong, I must tell you I realized that everything he taught me really didn't work for me—it worked only for Bruce. Or for me if I had Bruce to inspire me.

Stirling Silliphant

Bruce's instruction was given in an almost off-hand manner. When he said, "The arm is solid but not rigid," it didn't make sense to me. They were just words spoken in the middle of a lesson.

Joe Hyams

One of the most important things for any JKD instructor to do is to protect the students against his own influence.

Chris Kent

It is true that when he conceived JKD for the first time, it was a style and the Jun Fan Gung Fu Institute was the place where we trained in JKD. But after six or seven months he stopped calling it a style—and that's where I think people get confused.

Dan Inosanto

The arts influencing the Jun Fan kickboxing phase were diverse in structure and origin. Western boxing. Thai boxing, savate, northern and southern gung-fu kicking, sikaran, modified wing chun, among others, were used.

Tim Tackett

Bruce's first-generation students have already changed how they interpret JKD as compared to how they interpreted it when they were younger. They are adapting to their own changes in fitness, speed, and power.

Cass Magda

My fondest memory of Bruce was that we would go to various schools around Oakland.

Leo T. Fong

This is just personal opinion, but he probably perceived that wing chun techniques no longer fit into the direction he was going—by that I mean the JKD structure.

Ted Wong

One of the main concerns to many of us is that a lot of stuff being taught as JKD today would never work in a real situation.

Pete Jacobs

I went through a lot of very hard situations in my life, and at that time I had no respect or regard for myself. Bruce made me realize that I am a human being and I have equal rights.

Taky Kimura

Bruce was the most inspiring teacher I have ever had. His lectures were philosophy supported with action. His demonstrations were challenging and inspiring. His words of wisdom remain fresh in my mind.

Dan Lee

Because of Bob Bremer's JKD knowledge, I quickly found out that roughly 90 percent of all the things I was teaching years ago were inefficient. I had partially lost that "critical eye" that is JKD. I was exploring, researching, and trying many arts without using JKD as a filter to look at them.

Tim Tackett

The jeet kune do practiced today is not Lee's jeet kune do, but rather someone else's path.

Robert Chu

When his art started to change Bruce did add some new techniques, but basically, he modified what he had. So, technique-wise, his moves were the same, but with slight modifications.

Ted Wong

According to Bruce himself, and this is in his own writing, the physical elements of Jeet Kune Do are comprised of three arts, all of which he modified: fencing, Western boxing, and wing chun.

Jerry Poteet

A lot of Bruce Lee's words became misinterpreted slogans that were used as a foundation to disrespect other styles. It is not good to eliminate respect for our traditions and cultures because they are part of ourselves.

Ted Lucaylucay

I haven't disregarded the original material taught by Bruce Lee; I still teach it and believe in it. Bruce's techniques form the nucleus or the foundation upon which we can build.

Larry Hartsell

At the Kali Academy the students used to spar very often and very hard. It was a testing ground. A lot of people left because of the hard sparring.

Richard Bustillo

The whole idea Bruce had in mind for the demonstration was recruiting students for the school— and it worked because many kenpo students began training with him.

Bob Bremer

I came up with a phrase that sums it all up for myself and my JKD Unlimited students. "If you want to learn how to fight, you must practice fighting, against someone who is fighting back!" That is exactly what Bruce Lee did. What changed Jun Fan Gung Fu to Jeet Kune Do was not an evolution of technique; it was an evolution of training methods,

Burt Richardson

The training was in Jeet Kune Do—it was not called "Jun Fan Gung Fu" or "JKD Concepts." My first certificate reads, "Jeet Kune Do."

Tim Tackett

I went to Dan's house and after a two-hour conversation, which took place while the JKD class was going on, he invited me to start training. It was the coolest day of my life.

Chris Kent

I couldn't maintain that weight without taking the weight gain powder and hitting the weights three-times a week. Bruce had me running with him and taking vitamins to improve my performance.

Ted Wong

It is important to realize that there are various pockets touched by Bruce Lee, and each one seems to be under the assumption that they, and only they, have the ultimate in terms of his knowledge. I am referring to the Seattle, San Francisco and Los Angeles groups. The fact is that Bruce Lee died when he was 32 years old and was still learning His own personal technique was in a continuous state of refinement.

John Steven Soet

For Bruce Lee to compete in a karate tournament would be akin to asking Albert Einstein to enter a high school spelling bee. Must we all work in restaurants to become chefs, or can't a woman be a stone fox unless she wins a beauty contest?

Paul Vunak

I think I stopped being able to do the things Bruce taught me the minute Bruce left for Hong Kong. There's something about a man who makes you believe in yourself. It's a very special power that only a master has. Bruce made you excel by making you believe in the impossible.

Stirling Silliphant

Along the way I persuaded Stirling Silliphant to share the cost of lessons because Bruce was quite expensive. We worked out three or four times a week in the driveway of my home over a period of three years.

Joe Hyams

Bruce understood that training serves as the trigger mechanism for the internal process of discovery and self-knowledge.

Chris Kent

In the beginning, Bruce's goal was to attain perfection in fighting. He developed his system and called it Jeet Kune Do. Later on, he realized that the real purpose of training and studying the martial arts was for self-improvement, and the fighting skills were just a by-product.

Dan Inosanto

JKD is personal expression and highly individualistic. I think it will evolve, as the practitioner needs to evolve to become more functional.

Cass Magda

Bruce was extremely honest both with other people and himself. That made him realize what he could and couldn't do, allowing him to set realistic goals.

Pete Jacobs

At one time Bruce and I were talking about starting a chain of schools in the United States, but later on we decided against it.

Taky Kimura

Bruce was the only person I have met who was able to demonstrate these Chinese principles of gentleness, softness, and water principles in action.

Dan Lee

Since I am an educator by profession, I've always believed that the purpose of teaching is to give people a "detector," so they can look at something and see by themselves if it is good or not.

Tim Tackett

I've been hurting for many years seeing people who have been misrepresenting Bruce Lee's art and teachings. I'm sorry if I offend anyone, but this is how I feel.

Ted Wong

Now, I see people using wind-up rear kicks and strikes, and calling it Jeet Kune Do, or two and three parries before a hit. It just astonishes me that they think it's Bruce's art.

Jerry Poteet

Some false JKD instructors were capitalizing on Bruce Lee's name and the Jeet Kune Do art while we were starving or "running in the red" like Dan Inosanto.

Ted Lucaylucay

We used to go to his house to train, and to book- stores to find old books about boxing or fencing. One day he spent $500 on one old boxing book published in the 17th or 18th century.

Larry Hartsell

Most people just want that piece of paper. They want the certification. I have a very stringent set of standards and programs that everybody has to follow.

Richard Bustillo

Bruce was looking for a handful of people to be the nucleus of his group. He was planning to give us special attention, but the group kind of thinned out—and I guess he felt bad about it.

Bob Bremer

I often went to Bruce's house in Culver City. At this point, we were working out three or four times a week.

Stirling Silliphant

The curious thing is that Bruce Lee also addressed bias in his letter to Wong Shun Leong when writing about his prejudices being wrong. He wrote, "Jeet Kune Do is only a name. The most important thing is to avoid having bias in the training."

Burt Richardson

Although Inosanto states that Taky as his senior, is the head of the system, Inosanto is widely recognized as the most knowledgeable in that he spent the most time with Lee before his death. Therefore, he became the most sought-after instructor.

John Steven Soet

Bruce Lee evolved to an uncommon level of skill in both martial arts and life. His ideas were a result of accommodating (not accumulating) all Ways, hence being bound by no Way. However, he had a foundation for what he did.

Paul Vunak

I told Bruce a little about my past and said I wanted to resume studying. Bruce nodded and asked me to demonstrate some of the techniques I thought I had mastered.

Joe Hyams

One day when I turned up to train, I was given Full Instructor Certificates in both the Jun Fan Martial Arts (Jeet Kune Do) and Filipino Kali/Escrima. There was no big elaborate ceremony. It was, "Here you go." And I said, "Oh, that's cool." And then I put them in my bag and worked out.

Chris Kent

We can say that at a high level of the art, JKD is highly individualized for each person. But herein lies the danger—some may think that their personal, partial segment is the only true JKD.

Dan Inosanto

I think Lee also realized the American market liked sizzle and flash, so he jazzed up wing chun with such trappings, while still retaining wing chun's functional essence.

Robert Chu

Everyone is different and this makes teaching everyone different, but Bruce left valuable information and a great structure for the student to eventually develop on their own.

Pete Jacobs

Bruce didn't have the tunnel-vision approach of the classic gung-fu man.

Taky Kimura

Many people cross-train in different styles unheard of 30 years ago. Many train today with equipment like focus gloves, kicking shields, Thai pads, et cetera which many styles did not use before. The standard of realism has changed. JKD ideas such as totality, full contact realism, absorb what is useful, et cetera are part of every martial artist's vocabulary.

Cass Magda

Bruce was very straightforward, and some people didn't like that. My relationship with him was one of a friend and teacher. He was very open and sincere with me all the time.

Dan Lee

JKD didn't end with Bruce Lee in Los Angeles, but JKD is not adding other disciplines to the art either. The key is having an understanding of how to stick to the principles.

Tim Tackett

Bruce didn't have any plans on how to preserve his JKD because he was not planning to die!

Ted Wong

What has happened to Jeet Kune Do is just as much my responsibility as any other of Bruce's students. That is why I am actively teaching again.

Jerry Poteet

Many of those who were telling me that teaching Jeet Kune Do in a commercial studio would "ruin the art" and that they would "never do it," went crazy selling books, videotapes, and giving JKD seminars around the world.

Ted Lucaylucay

I had a lot of hostility in me. Basically, Bruce channeled that hostility into martial arts and changed my personality for the better.

Larry Hartsell

Many people think JKD is our system, when in fact it was Bruce's personal system. We used the Jun Fan gung fu name because no one wanted to use Jeet Kune Do to capitalize on Bruce's name.

Richard Bustillo

At the "kwoon" in Los Angeles Chinatown, all the students were given membership cards. Mine was number 105 because all the numbers started with the number "100" which happened to be Dan Lee's card number.

Bob Bremer

Bruce took me to a place and had me buy some weight-gain powder, a basic barbell set, and a bench press. He set up a personal program for me.

Ted Wong

Bruce Lee's kickboxing phase began in 1965 when he moved to Los Angeles from Oakland to pursue his acting career. Prior to that time, he was Jun Fan/wing chun oriented.

Tim Tackett

The most important evolution for me, though, concerns the principle of pressure testing. Bruce Lee changed from Jun Fan Gung Fu to Jeet Kune Do because of what he discovered once he started sparring hard.

Burt Richardson

Dan told us that while he had made a promise to Bruce not to use the name commercially, we hadn't, so we were free to use the name if we wanted to. But it was still always in the back of our minds.

Chris Kent

During Bruce Lee's life, it was understood that he was the undisputed master of the system. His wishes were observed, his inconsistencies tolerated. People didn't mind paying to learn a specific fighting system called jeet kune do and reading that it was neither an art nor a style. They were learning something unique – a streamlined, ingeniously simplistic modern system with modern training methods only a privileged few were permitted to train under his three practicing instructors, Dan Inosanto, Taky Kimura and James Lee.

John Steven Soet

I recall, in my training under Dan Inosanto, Dan telling me that in his observations of Bruce Lee in confrontations, the straight blast would inevitably come at some point, particularly if Bruce took his opponent seriously.

Cass Magda

In JKD, because we don't have a black belt, a lot of people ask, "How long will it take for me to become certified? How long will it take for me to become an instructor?"

Chris Kent

One reason for Bruce Lee's incredible ability was simply due to the fact that he NEVER lost that lust to improve. To further complement that mentally . . . he despised the concept of having "belts."

Paul Vunak

Bruce believed in giving the student experiences he could grow from. What the student absorbs from that experience is pretty much up to him.

Dan Inosanto

The last time I saw Bruce was in '71 or '72, right when he was going to make "Big Boss". I have the last letter he sent me which said "things are going my way. When it rains it pours". He hadn't changed much. He was still obsessed with the martial arts.

Leo T. Fong

When I used to box, I was quite hostile. I enjoyed using my boxing skills to score on my opponent.

Dan Lee

Joe Hyams and I found it fascinating that when we were blindfolded and followed Bruce's instructions we felt the power of this defense. It was almost impossible for anyone to force his way through to the target, into your face or into your body.

Stirling Silliphant

Some weeks later a friend arranged for me to meet Bruce at my home. I asked Bruce if he was taking private students. Bruce said, "Occasionally," and asked me if I'd had any previous training.

Joe Hyams

Guys like Ted Wong, Bob Bremer, Dan Lee, etc... were "doing JKD" and "being JKD" under Bruce. They never thought about teaching openly. Some have never taught. They were happy with training under Bruce and they have really worthwhile JKD insights and "oral traditions."

Cass Magda

Bruce made so many changes and adaptations to what he learned in Hong Kong that he couldn't call what he was doing wing chun.

Pete Jacobs

What we were doing was called Jeet Kune Do. The school itself was known as the Jun Fan Gung Fu Institute.

Chris Kent

Dan Inosanto was among a headful of students that Bruce taught privately in his living room between 1965 and 1966. In late '66, Bruce began to conduct small semi-public gung-fun classes behind Wayne Chan's Pharmacy in Los Angeles' Chinatown. In 1967 the Chinatown school on College Street was opened. It was during this time that Bruce Lee's kickboxing era flourished.

Tim Tackett

We were both Oriental and they say that "blood is thicker than water." I guess Bruce needed someone that he could trust and depend on for more than simply gung-fu training.

Taky Kimura

How are you going to teach somebody to express himself? You can help him, and you can teach him, but his personal expression will come from him, not from you.

Tim Tackett

JKD is what Bruce Lee was practicing and teaching during his lifetime. He developed the art based on some important philosophical and physical principles— that is what everyone has to learn as their strong foundation.

Ted Wong

You can't do whatever and call it "My JKD." You are doing Bruce Lee's art of Jeet Kune Do, or you're not doing it at all.

Jerry Poteet

Like it or not, you have to face reality and JKD has become a style and it is part of the business world of martial arts.

Ted Lucaylucay

Grappling arts were very popular in the America's early sporting years. Everything goes full circle.

Larry Hartsell

My training in Jeet Kune Do began in the mid-'60s. I was one of the students at the original Chinatown *kwoon* in Los Angeles. I was also one of those chosen to work with Bruce privately at his house.

Richard Bustillo

You would go to Bruce's house, and he'd have a motion picture camera set up and he'd be watching Jack Dempsey, Jess Willard, et cetera, with a mirror. He'd turn them around and put them in a right-hand stance instead of a left.

Bob Bremer

Much of the art of Jeet Kune Do is hacking away at the inessentials. That is refinement. But if you want to create a magnificent sculpture like Michelangelo's David, you must start with a very large piece of marble.

Burt Richardson

I stopped training because I got married and things changed for me significantly. Later on, I took tai chi under Dan Lee and because of him I went back to Dan Inosanto's backyard school, since the Chinatown school was closed by then.

Pete Jacobs

After Bruce Lee's death in 1973, Mr. Inosanto, Bruce's protégé, continued to cultivate and refine the original process by which he and Bruce developed jeet kune do. This process is not static, it is dynamic in nature and continues to evolve, as was Bruce's intention.

Paul Vunak

When Bruce Lee died suddenly, he left a lot of loose threads. Among them was leadership. He really didn't have a lieutenant per se. If anyone could be considered a forceful leader, it was James Lee, who died before Bruce. Ted Wong did not practice or teach to the public, so he was not involved in anything political. Therefore, the mantle of leadership passed to two men—Dan Inosanto and Taky Kimura.

John Steven Soet

Had I worked out directly with him at first it would have been futile. So this was one of the reasons he put Joe Hyams and me together. He coached us in what he wanted us to learn. It became a very rewarding and beautiful experience and I remember it the way Joe does—with great respect and warm nostalgia.

Stirling Silliphant

One of the things with JKD is that while there is a natural form of training progression there are no iron-clad rules of what has to be taught.

Chris Kent

With Lee's teachings now interpreted in so many diverse (and often opposite) ways, it complicates things and makes politics run rampant.

Robert Chu

The JKD family has the material handed down directly from Bruce Lee. He started the term "Jeet Kune Do," but he was sorry he coined it because it was a personal experience. He felt the term was limiting the art and that it confined it in a way.

Dan Inosanto

When you look at what the guys in Oakland have and the guys in Chinatown have, it isn't really all that different. There is a lot of common ground there.

Cass Magda

The misconception most people have is that they mistake the movie persona with the real Bruce Lee. Simply put, Bruce was a human being who was hooked on martial arts, and wanted the world to see what he knew.

Leo T. Fong

Bruce's knowledge was limited at that time, but the basic principles of economy of motion, simplicity, and directness that he was teaching in Seattle were the same that he taught later on in the Oakland and Los Angeles schools.

Taky Kimura

In class Bruce was very serious. He demanded total attention. We had a relaxed but serious atmosphere. He felt he had so much to offer that he wasn't comfortable with people joking around.

Dan Lee

We just called it "Jeet Kune Do" like we did in the backyard classes, because that's what it was—JKD.

Tim Tackett

The JKD philosophy is very liberating, but you have to be careful in order to use it properly— don't get lost in never ending, nonsensical research.

Ted Wong

Bruce saw that some of us were very dedicated, so he gave us supplementary programs. I realized that I was going to need an edge if I was to succeed in his art.

Jerry Poteet

The key to all this boils down to the common denominator called experience. The JKD main activity seeks experience because only by experiencing can he arrive at any sort of self-knowledge, self-understanding, and self-realization.

Cass Magda

The JKD Society was created to do what I was trying to do since 1982 with my JKD Association. Unfortunately, it didn't work.

Ted Lucaylucay

I met Bruce through Dan Inosanto in 1964. I was training at Ed Parker's school when Dan Inosanto and Bruce walked in. We were sparring and after class, Bruce asked me to spar with him. I couldn't touch him.

Larry Hartsell

Dan told us, "Look, if these people who aren't trained or qualified are using it, then you guys who *are* qualified should start using the name."

Chris Kent

I used to teach the basic probation class where I weeded out the undesirables by giving them very hard training sessions. We wanted to know how the person was as a student. Inosanto was teaching the advanced classes.

Richard Bustillo

Inosanto had been training under Bruce since 1964 but the Chinatown school opened in February 1967. Before that, Bruce was training Tony Hum, Inosanto, and Wayne Chan in a Los Angeles pharmacy.

Bob Bremer

I had a strong inner desire to gain the ability to protect myself since enduring a terrible incident when I was 9. The predator was a large adult and the ordeal of being absolutely helpless while he continually threatened to kill me if I didn't do what he wanted created that desire for self-defense skills.

Burt Richardson

There's this common misconception that Bruce simply took the "best" of various arts and combined them to create his own art. This is essentially wrong.

Chris Kent

Throughout the years since Lee's death, training methods from other martial arts such as many Thai, savate, pentak silat, etc., have been synthesized into the Jun Fan curriculum so improve constantly.

Tim Tackett

The foil in Fencing seemed to me light years ahead of the other two weapons—it provided the same reason I fell in love with Bruce Lee's Jeet Kune Do—"The Way of the Intercepting Fist."

Stirling Silliphant

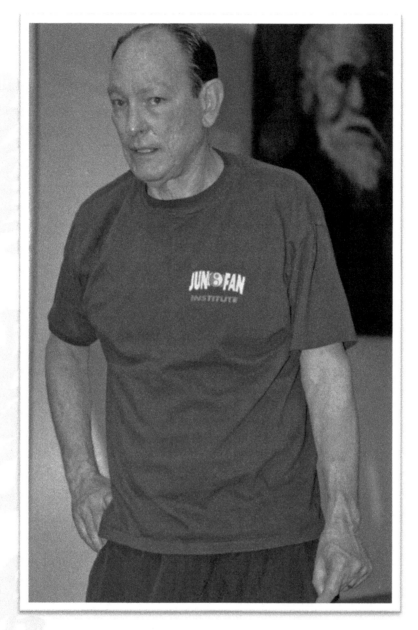

We have Bruce Lee's curriculum and progression in JKD. The art has a number of major theories that have to be totally understood.

Dan Inosanto

I first saw Bruce demonstrating at Ed Parker's tournament at the Long Beach Sports Arena in 1964. He walked onto the floor wearing a simple, black, tailor-made kung-fu uniform. He spoke quietly about Jeet Kune Do, demonstrated the one-inch punch, and then he performed full contact sparring with Danny Inosanto.

Joe Hyams

The Tao of Jeet Kune Do was an unfinished collection of his notes, from various sources, to explain the art of intercepting. Many take it to be *his* writing or *his* truth. They mistake "the finger pointing to the moon," as the moon.

Robert Chu

I had studied several other martial arts since I was 13, but nothing seemed to have everything I was looking for. At the time I really wasn't even sure what I was hoping to find. So I was just looking around and searching for something.

Chris Kent

The first time I met Dan Inosanto was in 1978 in Aspen, Colorado, where he was teaching a summer camp. I told him I'd like to really learn this. He said it would be better if I came to L.A.

Cass Magda

I met Bruce shortly after he arrived in Seattle. I was 38 and almost old enough to be his father. I met him through Jesse Glover who was Bruce's first student in Seattle.

Taky Kimura

Bruce researched different martial arts in order to absorb principles and concepts of doing things, and in the end, he developed his own "way." This is the reason why Jeet Kune Do is not an accumulation of techniques from different styles.

Pete Jacobs

Immediately after their first encounter, Dan became Bruce Lee's student. Over the next nine years, both Bruce and Dan literally dissected and synthesized every martial art and philosophy salient to the concept of JKD...street fighting!

Paul Vunak

Bruce said that "Truth cannot be perceived until we come to fully understand ourselves and our potential."

Dan Lee

Jeet Kune Do had all the push, yet no one wanted to make this work for the good of the art itself.

Ted Lucaylucay

During my stay in Taiwan as a member of the Air Force. I studied hsing-I, which is an internal system but also very effective for fighting. I had also training in other arts such as tai chi, northern Shaolin, southern Shaolin and white crane gung-fu. I had a black belt in karate as well.

Tim Tackett

It was in 1964 at the Ed Parker Internationals in Long Beach when my teacher Ed Parker introduced me to Bruce.

Dan Inosanto

Wing chun is the system Bruce studied under Yip Man in Hong Kong, and it helped him to understand, very clearly, certain combat principles such as simplicity and directness,

Ted Wong

Many of Bruce's students in the Chinatown School were kenpo students at Ed Parker's school. I was one of the first two students admitted to Bruce's school in Chinatown.

Jerry Poteet

I began in 1958 in judo, but I also trained in wrestling. I was fascinated by Japanese karate at that time, so I started to train shotokan under Hidetaka Nishiyama. Later on, I began studying kenpo karate under Ed Parker at his school in Santa Monica.

Larry Hartsell

We were using the term "Jun Fan gung fu" when we were talking about Bruce's art, and the phonies were using the Jeet Kune Do name! We were true JKD practitioners, so we didn't need to advertise and use the name. Only the uneducated announced their schools as JKD schools.

Richard Bustillo

Bruce described JKD as "bare essential street-fighting." Unfortunately, I don't think that a very high percentage of people have a clue about what real combat is.

Bob Bremer

Bruce Lee started with Wing Chun and was familiar with a few other methods. After he moved to Seattle, he began to evolve, changing the Wing Chun structure and adding techniques, thus creating Jun Fan Gung Fu. When he started sparring hard in Los Angeles, he found that he "had a lot of prejudices, but those ideas were wrong". This is when he changed the name to Jeet Kune Do. It was a new direction based on evidence gleaned from sparring many types of opponents.

Burt Richardson

Many say that wing chun gave Lee the tools to make a sculpture—but Ed Parker said that without the ability of Bruce Lee, you could sculpt all day and come out with nothing. Parker realized you need a system.

Robert Chu

In 1964, Dan Inosanto first met Bruce Lee. At that time, Mr. Inosanto already held black belts in several other arts, and was a world-class martial artist in his own right. Dan's athletic ability was and is at an uncommon level.

Paul Vunak

My whole desire to become involved in the martial arts stemmed from my early romantic readings and my love affair with fencing, which sport, incidentally, Joe Hyams also embraced.

Stirling Silliphant

Although JKD isn't treated as a style and each JKD person might express the art in a different way, there are still certain peculiarities of movements that result in a similarity of the art's practitioners.

Chris Kent

In small informal groups like your garage no one cares if you aren't using the right terms—it really doesn't matter because you read between the lines. But when you go out in public it should be clear and specific, so you don't have to read between the lines.

Cass Magda

I had a little judo training in the service, pretty much on my own. Then when I left the Air Force, I trained kenpo karate under Ed Parker for over four years, and then went into training with Bruce Lee in the Chinatown school.

Pete Jacobs

Bruce realized that it was an important part of the totality in combat, but not the only part of it as he emphasized during his days in Seattle where he taught wing chun.

Taky Kimura

I've been studying and evolving as a martial artist. Not being in the spotlight doesn't mean that I haven't been actively training, teaching, and learning.

Dan Lee

If JKD had any one thing that it was not strong at, it would be the grappling.

Tim Tackett

I don't know if I was Bruce's protege, but I had a great relationship with him both as a student and as a friend. As friends we spent a lot of time together going to bookstores, watching movies, et cetera.

Ted Wong

Bruce was so particular about what and whom he taught, and yet, Jeet Kune Do has become the McDonald's of martial arts.

Jerry Poteet

I never met Bruce, but I witnessed the famous demonstration he gave at the Long Beach Internationals in 1964.

Ted Lucaylucay

Bruce sacrificed everything to become the best martial artist on earth. And you have to respect that.

Bob Bremer

We used to do a lot of heavy-bag training, air-shield drills, wing chun sensitivity drills, and trapping hands. Everything focused on being practical and functional in combat.

Larry Hartsell

Dan Inosanto was Bruce's assistant in Los Angeles and he has been instrumental in the discovery of my own JKD. I became his assistant at his backyard school in Carson, California, after Bruce closed down the Chinatown *kwoon*.

Richard Bustillo

I remember waking up from a nap and turning on the TV in 1973. It was on the news that Bruce had died. I couldn't believe it. I thought it was a joke.

Leo T. Fong

I will also mention that many people mistake Jun Fan Gung Fu for Jun Fan JKD. There are many aspects of the former that Bruce Lee realized were not so functional when he started sparring hard and therefore discarded them. Many truths were revealed once the scientific method was applied to Jun Fan Gung Fu.

Burt Richardson

Bruce Lee's original art was wing chun. After seeing certain limitations in wing chun (or any one art), the next obvious step was to investigate the principles, concepts, and techniques of various different arts. The process of this investigation is the very essence of JKD.

Paul Vunak

I had never taken any martial arts instruction before Bruce. But by the time I met Bruce I had read voluminously, everything I could get in the field: Chinese, Japanese, Korean techniques. But back then it was all theoretical material to me. It was my head only—not part of kinetic response.

Stirling Silliphant

Bruce Lee ultimately became his own teacher and did mostly self-training. But this was training with imagination, concentration, and intensity.

Chris Kent

I believe that my last meeting with Bruce was in May or June of 1973 when he came back to United States for a health exam because he blacked out while editing films in the cutting room in Hong Kong.

Dan Inosanto

Dan Inosanto used to say "lineage students" are like the horns on a bull and the rest of the students are like the hairs. There are only two horns but a lot of hairs!

Cass Magda

At that time a lot of Bruce's Chinatown school group were training with Ed Parker: Jerry Poteet, Bob Bremer, Steve Golden, Dan Lee and, of course, Dan Inosanto, who was also teaching for Ed Parker. It was a great time.

Pete Jacobs

Bruce used to come to Seattle because Linda's mother was living here. He used to call me in advance so I could take time away from work to be trained in the new things he was going into.

Taky Kimura

My immediate instructor under Ed Parker, Dan Inosanto, recommended me to Bruce Lee, who just happened to start a school in Los Angeles.

Dan Lee

Ed Parker said to another karate legend that Bruce was "walking death." Enough said. He was living proof of the idea of "daily decrease."

Tim Tackett

My roommate told me about *The Green Hornet* TV series. I began to watch the show and I became very interested in meeting him.

Ted Wong

Bruce's speed and power improved each time you saw him, but what was most impressive was his great awareness. By this I mean, he developed his visual, perceptual, and tactile awareness to such a height.

Jerry Poteet

Dan Inosanto was training a select group of people in his backyard at the time. Richard Bustillo, who was Inosanto's training partner, invited me to come down and train with them. It was May 1973.

Ted Lucaylucay

At that time, I was on leave from the Army before going to Vietnam, so I asked Bruce if I could train with him after my discharge. He said it was OK. We did train with Dan Inosanto on and off until I left to Vietnam.

Larry Hartsell

Our idea [Dan and me] was to promote the Filipino arts and share our experience and knowledge in Jeet Kune Do. We had a JKD class for some selected senior students.

Richard Bustillo

Bruce was always looking to see if there were any movements or secrets, he could discover from the old boxing movies.

Bob Bremer

I'm sure Bruce Lee would have added some important elements to his ground fighting if he had access to the current set of grapplers.

Burt Richardson

My friendship with Jimmy Lee began in 1960. I met him at a Siu Lum School, and we were both looking for the same thing-something that worked.

Leo T. Fong

Bruce Lee used to talk about the importance of "feeling" one's muscles throughout the range of motion, or to perceive whether or not they are tense or loose. Once the ability to monitor personal muscular contraction is accomplished, one can then make the proper neurological adjustments.

Paul Vunak

When I ultimately heard about Bruce, I wanted to meet him. At that late point in my life, I had decided that I wanted to become a little more physical. I wanted to study, but not out of any compulsion to enhance my posture of self-defense.

Stirling Silliphant

When I authorize someone to teach the art, I want the public to be assured that they're going to get the best quality instruction in Bruce's art and philosophy.

Chris Kent

Five decades ago, he was talking about things that most martial artists didn't understand and even fewer believed. Without mentioning names, I can say that his knowledge and skills were far beyond any martial artist of his time.

Dan Inosanto

For any individual's search, JKD is complete but never finished. As of this moment it's complete but tomorrow there might be something new we learn that will improve things.

Cass Magda

Some of us were invited by Ed Parker to go up to San Francisco for a tournament that the Castro brothers were preparing. He asked us if we wanted to meet Bruce so we said, "Of course!" We went to Oakland to James Y. Lee's house.

Pete Jacobs

Sometimes there are things that we don't understand today but that will become increasingly clear to us in time.

Taky Kimura

I attended his demonstration in Long Beach in 1964, and I was very impressed by his speed and power.

Dan Lee

Bruce Lee never wanted JKD to be a closed system, but he had a JKD structure, a JKD base, and certain JKD techniques.

Tim Tackett

Bruce was always fast to pick up on marital arts techniques, and by the early 1970s, his skill for both observation and execution had reached such a phenomenal level that very few people could keep up with him.

Ted Wong

Bruce knew that to be a good fighter you needed to reach your maximum potential psychologically as well as physically.

Jerry Poteet

I began training in judo but eventually I also trained in shito-ryu and shorin-ryu karate, kajukenbo under Tony Ramos, and praying mantis kung-fu before getting into JKD.

Ted Lucaylucay

Bruce's philosophy and the principles and concepts of Jeet Kune Do were something I always believed in from the first time I met him.

Richard Bustillo

One day Bruce said to me, "I want to teach you everything." I said, "Sure! You just want everyone to try out this old man!"

Bob Bremer

The sparring was pretty heavy, and it was a big focus of the training. The original Kali Academy felt more like a boxing gym than a martial arts dojo, so imagine 25 really tough fighters in that advanced class.

Burt Richardson

One must understand that a seminar serves as a vehicle for personal growth, and not a teaching credential. What one gets out of a seminar is dictated purely by their existing level, attitude (having an empty cup), rate of understanding and absorption, training intensity, etc. There should never be such a thing as an instructorship seminar, in which graduating from a two-day (or week-long) seminar entitles the participant to teach that art.

Paul Vunak

Bruce had a school in the Chinatown of Los Angeles. Very low profile. No exterior sign. You had to know its location in advance. And you had to be invited. You didn't just walk in off the street.

Stirling Silliphant

Don't take the material in Bruce's notes to be the Bible, to which nothing should ever be added or taken away and turn it into law. And don't just memorize the material and develop the ability to repeat it by rote.

Chris Kent

Bruce told me that he would use me as his dummy, and in exchange would train me in his system, at that time a devastating modified form of wing chun—Jeet Kune Do had not yet been conceived.

Dan Inosanto

It is important that people understand that a "JKD man" might not always be teaching "Jeet Kune Do."

Cass Magda

Bruce would start with some simple techniques and go from there— mainly lead hand and lead foot. He worked us on the proper use of the lead side. He didn't allow us to use the rear side of the body.

Pete Jacobs

Towards the end Bruce was really deviating from the Wing Chun. He was moving more like a "refined" kickboxer.

Leo T. Fong

I think it's important to go through the pieces that Bruce discarded, study them, and learn them to get up to that point, because it was an ongoing process of "shedding away the nonessentials."

Taky Kimura

When Dan Inosanto introduced me to Bruce, I could perceive that he was very cautious about who I was. But when I told him about my martial arts background, he became very interested in having me.

Dan Lee

Bruce never wanted JKD to be a style—but 50 years ago the term "style" was something very closed and had a negative connotation.

Tim Tackett

Bruce and I were from similar cultural backgrounds and we both thought in the same mother tongue language, so we were able to communicate on a more personal level. We were also very close in height, weight and body size and we shared similar ranges of body motions and degrees of flexibility.

Ted Wong

I met Bruce for the first time prior to Chinatown at James Lee's house in Oakland, California. Here was this young, small guy, I really wasn't all that impressed with his appearance.

Jerry Poteet

Dan Inosanto had a well-equipped gym. He invested a lot of money in it and I remember him telling me that he was "running in red," but that he was doing it as "a labor of love for the art."

Ted Lucaylucay

Jeet kune do was Lee's personal research and development vehicle to make his wing chun come alive. That is why he eventually regretted coining the term "jeet kune do."

Robert Chu

Bruce was very Chinese. He was an all-around neat guy, but he was stuck on martial arts. If you wanted to talk about anything else, forget it!

Bob Bremer

I went to watch a class at the original Kali Academy space in 1979. Sifu Dan (we usually referred to him as Sifu at that time) was teaching and it was absolutely amazing. I had seen karate before and was certainly intrigued, but here we had a group of people moving smoothly and athletically, wearing T-shirts and sweatpants while they hit the mitts and then each other (during sparring).

Burt Richardson

Twenty years ago, the idea of one instructor flying to a different school (actually teaching their students) was unheard of. Bruce Lee popularized the idea that no one art has it all and instructors all over the country became more open minded to this concept.

Paul Vunak

Bill Dozier put me in touch with someone who gave me Bruce's phone number. I called Bruce. I said, "My name is Stirling Silliphant. I've been looking for you for three months. I want to study with you." Bruce said, "Well, I don't really teach. I only have one or two private students."

Stirling Silliphant

Bruce's notes should be viewed as guideposts or directional aids that can help lead an individual to their own self-expression in martial arts. They're signposts that will help guide a person to the correct path toward learning how to make good use of themselves.

Chris Kent

When I gave a demonstration with Bruce, he said "Just do what I tell you and we'll make up the demonstration from there." He'd be talking, then all of a sudden, he'd say, "Punch or a kick. I'll take care of it. Just punch or kick." At first I didn't like it, then I got used to the way he demonstrated.

Dan Inosanto

The people look at what Dan Inosanto is investigating at the time, and they take that as the way. He's so good at relating the principles of JKD to other arts that you can misunderstand that whatever art he was showing fits into JKD.

Cass Magda

To be honest, I believe he wanted to find out if what he found true for himself could work on somebody else. I guess he was experimenting with us to a certain extent; trying to see if we, as students, could deliver what he modified and created.

Pete Jacobs

Bruce's approach was very revolutionary in the mid-'60s and many people weren't ready to understand what he was talking about.

Taky Kimura

After two months Bruce began the serious training. This was a very Chinese mentality. It's a traditional way of testing a student's persistence and dedication.

Dan Lee

Dan Inosanto was being constantly required to teach Jeet Kune Do, but he was not really happy with that idea.

Tim Tackett

Bruce once described his martial arts efforts by comparing them to the work of a sculptor, a JKD practitioner does not keep adding techniques, but hacks away at the unessentials in his art so that the true spirit of the martial arts is expressed.

Ted Wong

I left the Inosanto Academy in 1975 to open my own school because I realized that a lot of things were going to change.

Ted Lucaylucay

I consider myself a JKD practitioner, pressure testing everything in my lifelong quest for constant, practical improvement, but without limiting myself to what Bruce Lee did in his lifetime. I follow the decree of "Using no way as way, having no limitation as limitation." That is why I call my approach JKD Unlimited.

Burt Richardson

Bruce Lee and Dan Inosanto were developing JKD after Bruce discovered that straight wing chun had certain limitations, both investigated every art they could get their hands on over a nine-year period.

Paul Vunak

We have no idea what Bruce would be studying or doing. We could assume, based upon what we have learned about his dedication and pursuit of excellence, that he would be keeping up with the latest developments in the fields of martial arts, fitness, and entertainment.

Chris Kent

Bruce always was around the top people in the martial arts scene, and I honestly doubt he had anyone who could give him a decent workout.

Pete Jacobs

The art of Jeet Kune Do was developed by Bruce while he was living in Los Angeles. I can say that it was the product of many years of martial arts research.

Taky Kimura

In combat, Bruce used to emphasize the "broken rhythm" so we had to be aware of whatever pace our partner was using in sparring.

Dan Lee

Taky Kimura was teaching in Seattle, but he was teaching a modified version of wing chun, which is what Bruce Lee taught him during his days in Tacoma.

Tim Tackett

I remember that during the period when he was living in Oakland, he went back to the Orient for a while. He said, "If I decide to stay in the States, I will teach you. If I don't, go to James Lee." He really trusted both men very much.

Dan Inosanto

When I first began with Inosanto it was just Jeet Kune Do, the art and philosophy of Bruce Lee. Later in the early '80s, mostly due to the seminars' demand for technique, JKD became separated into "Jun Fan Gung Fu," meaning the techniques of the physical art, and "JKD Concepts."

Cass Magda

The three people who helped Bruce make and modify equipment were James Lee, George Lee, and later in Los Angeles, Herb Jackson.

Ted Wong

Aside from Steve McQueen and maybe one or two others, Bruce was not really into teaching private lessons. In order to discourage Hollywood dilettantes, he charged a great deal of money for each hour of instruction.

Stirling Silliphant

To really spread, the art had to be taught in seminars and there had to be more instructors. I really doubt if all them are really qualified to teach JKD, but that's another matter.

Ted Lucaylucay

It was Shannon Lee who had the brilliant suggestion to call the art that Bruce Lee did himself after moving to Los Angeles Jun Fan JKD. The era before would be described as Jun Fan Gung Fu. What a simple, easy to understand way of delineating between the approaches.

Burt Richardson

JKD is a synthesis of one's personal power by the continuing improvement of one's own efficiency, and the continuing educational process. Eclecticism on the other hand is, to randomly accumulate styles and techniques. Since most styles take a lifetime to accommodate, the eclectic martial artist is generally forever trapped in the role of beginner.

Paul Vunak

I read two articles about Jeet Kune Do, one written by Bruce Lee, and the other by Dan Inosanto. Something about JKD just seemed to strike a chord with me and I thought, "This is what I want to learn."

Chris Kent

Bruce and I went round and round as far as the curriculum for Chinatown school. We finally did it and he allowed me to have some input. Of course, he was controlling everything and advising me what to teach and what not to.

Dan Inosanto

I thought the outside of the kali Academy didn't look like much because it was in this warehouse industrial area, but once inside it was huge. The place had an aura and energy to it. Brick walls, equipment everywhere—sort of a boxing gym vibe.

Cass Magda

After I left Dan Inosanto's school because of my work schedule, I really wanted to keep training and I figured that if I had a small group of people, I could keep practicing what I knew.

Pete Jacobs

To me, Jeet Kune Do is yin/yang philosophy in action and from my tai chi studies I realized where Bruce's thoughts came from.

Dan Lee

I remember that on one occasion James Lee was visiting the *kwoon* in Los Angeles and was watching us work out. After the training session, Bruce came to me, put his hand on my shoulder and said, "You know what James said about you? He said that you really got it." I was very proud that James said that about me.

Dan Lee

The assistant to a Tai chi instructor in Chinatown asked me if I knew Bruce Lee. When we answered "yes," he said that his assistant, Dan Inosanto, was teaching in his backyard because Bruce Lee just closed down the *kwoon*. This person was Dan Lee.

Tim Tackett

Bruce was teaching us how to look at ourselves to improve individually. He always tried to condition the students' minds by giving a proper example of how to train.

Ted Wong

Inosanto and Bustillo decided to open the Kali Academy in Torrance, California, a few months after Bruce passed away. The students began to fluctuate and there were visitors from all over the world looking for the art of Jeet Kune Do.

Ted Lucaylucay

Bruce Lee felt the chest offers the best signs of the opponent's attack. One should gaze into the chest without fixing the eyes. "You should know the color shirt your opponent is wearing without reading the fine print."

Paul Vunak

When we are talking about Jun Fan JKD, what Bruce Lee did himself towards the end of his life, each of the afore-mentioned teachers displayed their own way of teaching it, meaning each approach is different. But there are far more similarities than many think.

Burt Richardson

I got a hold of Dan's telephone number and called him—and called and called. Finally, after about two months of phone calls he invited me to come down to his backyard gym to talk.

Chris Kent

The Chinatown school started in February and in May he transferred the teaching responsibilities to me. He started me off there, watching for the first three months. But after the third month, he would come once a week or so and check it out.

Dan Inosanto

The day after my graduation in 1979, I took a plane to California and began my adventure with him. My family thought I was crazy but that was what I wanted. I haven't looked back since.

Cass Magda

Students dropping from class—it was good for us [the ones staying] because I don't believe that what Bruce was trying to convey to us could be taught to a class of 30 or 40 students.

Pete Jacobs

Bruce was 17 years old at that time and came to stay with Ping and Ruby Chow who were longtime friends of his father and who owned a restaurant where Bruce was supposed to work as a waiter.

Taky Kimura

In Oakland, James Lee was teaching something in-between, because "Jeet Kune Do" as such was created and developed during Bruce's days in Los Angeles.

Tim Tackett

Bruce was privately teaching Dan Inosanto and Tony Hum at a pharmacy in Chinatown, Los Angeles. My roommate knew the place, so I went a couple of times and just sort of stayed in the background and watched him.

Ted Wong

Teaching in backyards and garages had been a major tradition in Jeet Kune Do. The times were changing, and I felt it was necessary to adapt to the new circumstances.

Ted Lucaylucay

In the style of Wing Chun, an art known for trapping, I have seen students who have spent five to ten years practicing their style and who have yet to learn how to trap.

Paul Vunak

Basically, he shut down all of his schools, not just the Los Angeles Chinatown school. I couldn't tell you the exact reason.

Chris Kent

As far as other martial artists training with Bruce, I watched him test his knowledge and skill. He always kept records on whom he was teaching. I don't know why he did it, I can only guess.

Dan Inosanto

Jeet Kune Do has become the Tower of Babel. Most cannot understand the other when Inosanto talks about JKD!

Cass Magda

In the beginning of the LA school the group was quite big, maybe 30 people or so, but it fluctuated a lot. Most of the students dropped out after a while because they couldn't deal with the intensity of the workouts.

Pete Jacobs

I can honestly say that if Bruce felt you were trustworthy, he was very unselfish about his teachings.

Taky Kimura

Bruce viewed unarmed combat as a science and investigated it as such.

Chris Kent

Bruce Lee had a very direct and honest way of both fighting I think Bruce was trying to men-tally and physically liberate his students from the traditional approach to martial arts.

Ted Wong

High-ranking martial artists were coming to the Kali Academy, and they were getting shattered by some senior students or beginners who had been there for only six months.

Ted Lucaylucay

and living. He developed his "watcher" in such a way that it continually tapped his personal power.

Paul Vunak

Bruce never wrote the term "JKD concepts." Just look at his personal writings and you will never find that name.

Ted Wong

The Green Hornet series hadn't started yet, and he didn't have a job. He was training me and a couple of guys more in Chinatown, right behind Wayne Chan's Pharmacy.

Dan Inosanto

What I found at the Kali Academy was what I expected from reading Inosanto's book, *"Jeet Kune Do: The Art and Philosophy of Bruce Lee"*. What was unexpected was the casual informality of the classes and culture of the school, yet everyone was so serious about their practice.

Cass Magda

Dan's backyard group was composed of some of the Bruce Lee students in Chinatown like Dan Lee, Bob Bremer, Richard Bustillo, Jerry Poteet. And others such as Ted Lucaylucay and later, Chris Kent.

Tim Tackett

"Bruce, I can get a bunch of kenpo guys together and you can start teaching a class. A little money won't harm you!" He accepted, and that was the beginning of the Jun Fan Gung Fu Institute in Los Angeles.

Dan Inosanto

When I watch Dan Inosanto move, his speed, his intensity, his power just never dull. He is quicker now than fifteen years ago!

Paul Vunak

High-ranking martial artists were coming to the Kali Academy, and they were getting shattered by some senior students or beginners who had been there for only six months.

Ted Lucaylucay

If an individual is looking outward for external rewards such as belts, et cetera, then they're relying on outside sources. And if they're looking for someone to give them all of the answers, then JKD is not for them.

Chris Kent

I saw guys at the Kali Academy dressed in T's and sweats slamming pads and each other and I said to myself, "This is the place! This is home!"

Cass Magda

Bruce was full of energy and somewhat flamboyant but on the other side he was a typical teenager. He spoke English with a British accent and at that time he stuttered a bit.

Taky Kimura

In 1970, Inosanto greatly influenced the curriculum by adding Filipino boxing (panantukan). There were two reasons for the addition: it added more sophistication to Western boxing and, it added the ability to drill realistically and combatively without each student bushing the other's face in every workout.

Tim Tackett

My roommate told me that Bruce was going to open a new school. It was not a public school. It was a private *kwoon,* and most of the students were coming from Ed Parker's kenpo school.

Ted Wong

Dan Inosanto, was teaching in his backyard because Bruce Lee just closed down the *kwoon.*

Tim Tackett

PHILOSOPHY

JKD is not a cultural art; it is a fighting method that requires rigorous testing by every single individual. "Research your own experience ". That's why Bruce Lee said that JKD was not for everyone. The majority of people in a relatively peaceful society don't see the need to endure that kind of training.

Burt Richardson

When one seeks a trainer in JKD, one should look carefully. Much depends on the people who trained the trainer. Ninety percent of the people practicing JKD now talk about "concept," but don't really know what it is. Their idea of "concept" had little or nothing to do with Bruce's art.

Ted Wong

Jeet kune do is Bruce Lee's personal philosophy, research, and development and reflects his own personal genius—jeet kune do was Bruce Lee's way of making his wing chun come alive.

Robert Chu

Bruce made me aware of the need to look into myself for direction, rather than depend on the outside. He said that in order for you to grow you have to find the cause of your own ignorance.

Leo T. Fong

It is wrong to say that a person who trained in the core jeet kune do concepts and learned the process of simplification and assimilation, and who then goes on to study and "absorb" other arts, is not pursuing a JKD path.

John Steven Soet

The oral tradition consists of knowledge taught but never written down. It's memorized by the practitioners and passed on personally. In Jeet Kune Do if you're not a lineage student then you're limited by the books, videos, seminars or whatever about the art.

Cass Magda

The primary difference between the training mentalities of the athlete and the martial artists is not some secret technique, but a training attitude that has no room for complacency.

Paul Vunak

Training is the process of preparation of a martial artist for the highest levels of performance. Therefore, the training process should be organized with a lot of foresight. The better the process, the better the results you should achieve.

Tim Tackett

Through his training and research, Bruce had developed what Dan refers to as "the discerning mind" and "the educated eye." His self-knowledge, training and research allowed him to analyze techniques and quickly discern what was a useful or efficient motion and what wasn't.

Chris Kent

As Bruce said, "Jeet Kune Do is a prescription for personal growth."

Dan Inosanto

Bruce considered the Yin/Yang philosophy so important that he designed his JKD emblem based on this principle.

Dan Lee

I cannot do what Bruce was doing. I'm not physically capable of delivering force the way he did, but I have a pretty good idea of how things work and how a person can make it work for themselves.

Pete Jacobs

During a conversation with Taky Kimura, Bruce said to Taky that "the *chi sao* was out." And *chi sao* was a very important part of the material taught to Taky by Bruce in Seattle

Ted Wong

I know that if Bruce were to come back tomorrow, and if he would once more give me the teaching he gave me before, in no time at all I would be doing the things I could do in those years now gone.

Stirling Silliphant

The problem was with me as a student rather than Bruce as a teacher. He was like Picasso, who had studied traditional painting and went through several stages of development and experimentation before arriving at a simplified technique.

Joe Hyams

Bruce was not into sport fighting—he was training for survival.

Bob Bremer

In my opinion, however, Bruce Lee was just a student of totality in combat – a goal that all martial artists seek. He simply stressed a concept of martial arts which came from his study of wing chun – interception.

Robert Chu

My goal is to transmit the essence of JKD without recourse to factions or political groups. To help instill in people the JKD attitude and serve as a "finger pointing to the moon," while I simultaneously learn and continue my own process of self-discovery.

Chris Kent

The thing that impressed me most about Bruce was not his skill, but his knowledge. Most people were impressed with his physical skill; but to me the most impressive aspect was his knowledge.

Dan Inosanto

My only advice would be: know yourself and be yourself— have an eye for what is functional and be adaptable. Keep an open mind. Stay cool and not get hung up on anything, whether it's philosophy, technique, training methods, or politics.

Cass Magda

The classes always started with several conditioning exercises for 30 or 40 minutes. For Bruce this was something extremely important.

Pete Jacobs

Self-training is extremely important in order to keep teaching properly. It is like a university teacher—after the classes he goes home and does more research, trying to keep up with new ideas and theories.

Taky Kimura

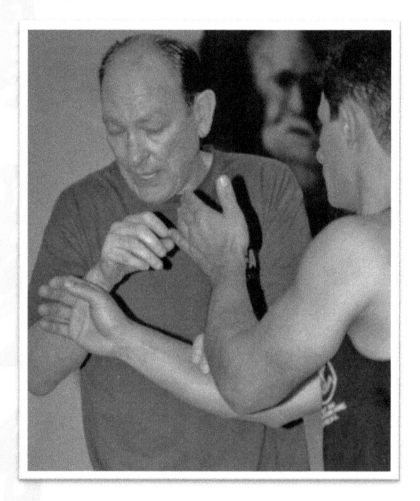

Bruce told me, "Always be teachable." I've been very busy studying the theories and practice of tai chi chuan and wing chun kung-fu.

Dan Lee

The real challenge of a JKD teacher is to teach the student to fish for himself—to become independent. That's what I like to do with my students.

Tim Tackett

Bruce used me as sparring partner for a lot of things he was developing at that time. That allowed me to reach a very high level quickly. I learned to stop his attacks, but I could never score on him.

Ted Wong

Bruce said that the purpose of Jeet Kune Do was to discover your own attitude, the essence of your being. Simple, yes. Easy, hell no!

Jerry Poteet

It's interesting that Dan was losing money with his backyard gym when he was in a perfect position to make millions from Jeet Kune Do and his association with Bruce Lee. But he refused to capitalize on his friendship and personal relationship with Bruce.

Ted Lucaylucay

In martial arts as well as in life, Bruce's legacy is to go beyond the concept of limited range or negative personal self-perception and use whatever is given to you to excel.

Larry Hartsell

Jeet Kune Do is Bruce Lee's personal martial art expression. He used certain philosophy and concepts that conformed to the guidelines of his investigation.

Richard Bustillo

I was totally convinced I was going to be a Bruce Lee student. I remember that at least five guys all changed schools at the same time. We jokingly called ourselves "The Turncoats" because we all switched over from Ed Parker and went there.

Bob Bremer

Everything I do is imbued with the JKD philosophy. I am interested primarily in street self-defense. Although I have become proficient in various combat sports, I modify them using JKD street-specific principles.

Burt Richardson

Coming with esoteric definitions culled from quotes (taken out of context) from specific philosophical tomes, some of them incompatible, and then redefining jeet kune do according to these terms, doesn't wash.

John Steven Soet

The principle is to find the top people available to you in each range and play the game with them. This is the best method I've ever seen for improving your skills and bringing yourself down to earth.

Paul Vunak

Bruce spoiled me forever because as long as he was present, as long as the master was around, I felt omnipotent. There wasn't anything I couldn't do.

Stirling Silliphant

If you went to study with Picasso without having his background, you would learn only his current style without an understanding of its background. And so, it was with me as a pupil of Bruce's.

Joe Hyams

When people really start to understand JKD, they see how it affects all other areas of their life, and that it's about so much more than just fighting.

Chris Kent

Bruce told me that I always had to respect Taky Kimura as my senior. Unfortunately, James Lee passed away before Bruce died. Bruce appreciated both men as true friends. They were older than him and Bruce really trusted them as human beings.

Dan Inosanto

For those teaching the art I would like to mention there must be a difference between teaching and practicing.

Taky Kimura

My goal is to produce committed, devoted individuals capable of teaching the art of Jeet Kune Do. To produce students who are dedicated to excellence and to walking the pathless path.

Cass Magda

Bruce's thinking was that if you're not in shape you're basically out of business—and he was right.

Pete Jacobs

The calm and patience of tai chi helped me to harmonize coordination between the body and mind. That slowness was very helpful to me in developing coordination and balance in my movements.

Dan Lee

The main concepts behind Bruce Lee's "real" JKD are derived from wing chun's motto: "Receive as the opponent comes, escort him when he leaves, rush in upon loss of contact."

Robert Chu

In a sense, at that point, Jeet Kune Do cannot be taught. It is self-expression.

Tim Tackett

Bruce used to say, "Ted, when you see me kick or punch, move away as fast as you can." You know, after thousands of times being hit you learn how to detect the smallest action!

Ted Wong

Bruce knew that the physical and philosophical go hand in hand, and without the philosophical underpinnings, it's not Jeet Kune Do.

Jerry Poteet

The Kali Academy was like a JKD fraternity because we used to spend most of our time training and talking about Jeet Kune Do. People were sleeping in sleeping bags and some would train rather than spend time with their family!

Ted Lucaylucay

Bruce's message was to express yourself and be able to move comfortably at any distance.

Larry Hartsell

My idea is to educate rather than certify people. I do not want to regulate people.

Richard Bustillo

I guess one of the reasons so many people dropped out was because he demanded too much—he suggested too much.

Bob Bremer

The basis for research and development is the scientific method. The scientific method is to create a hypothesis, test that hypothesis in a realistic environment, then observe the results of the test. The results are the results. It's not about what you would like the world to be like, it is about what it actually is.

Burt Richardson

Bruce Lee was an admirer of the late sage, J. Krishnamurti. Krishnaurti's last words were, "All of those years, and no one has gotten it." They could just as easily have been Bruce Lee's last words.

John Steven Soet

One's fighting ability depends on the quality of one's attribute, such as speed, power, coordination, footwork, etc. The major point I would like to project here is that each attribute requires a different time frame to maintain.

Paul Vunak

Bruce also used to teach us to rid our minds of extraneous thoughts. For instance, while talking to you he'd unexpectedly throw an orange at you, and he expected you—without looking or even being aware of it—just to catch it.

Stirling Silliphant

I was really unprepared for Bruce. Although mature in years, I wasn't mature enough in my ability to get the most from what he offered—and he offered a great deal.

Joe Hyams

JKD is a living, breathing thing. As such it has to remain in motion and in use to survive.

Chris Kent

Bruce firmly believed that the instructor was merely a guide, not a dictator, and that the teacher is the "pointer" of the truth, not the "giver" of the truth.

Dan Inosanto

Today we are likely to face an opponent in the street with a sophisticated martial arts background. Certainly, our minds should remain open enough to grow from this awareness and prepare ourselves.

Cass Magda

I guess all that conditioning training was also a way of testing if we were truly interested in learning what he had to offer. He didn't want to waste his time and effort.

Pete Jacobs

You must always try to develop your mind; you can be very strong, fast, and fit, but if you lack a strong mind your physical aspects will mean nothing in a real situation.

Taky Kimura

I believe jeet kune do was Lee's term for his path of research for making wing chun come alive – he focused on the core principle important to him – the timing and ability to intercept his opponent's motions.

Robert Chu

People wanted to learn the fighting techniques, but Bruce wanted to give us the basic physical training and check out our character at the same time.

Dan Lee

The JKD core can be taught. But the other side of the coin is that because JKD's highest level is self-expression, no teacher can teach you at this "post-graduate" level.

Tim Tackett

JKD became Bruce's personal expression in combat. And that's what it is.

Ted Wong

It pains me to see that Jeet Kune Do has degenerated in the public's mind to me as just "martial arts," a generic term to be applied to practically anything,

Jerry Poteet

Some insiders used to say, "JKD never loses." The truth of the matter, though, is that the style became more important than the individual because the style was preventing us from growing through the experience of competition.

Ted Lucaylucay

The artist must develop his own style and then pattern his strokes after his particular skills, even if he uses the same brush and canvas or "base system."

Larry Hartsell

The problem was that the kajukenbo system stays within the limits of the methods used in the style. You can't break away from those and express yourself totally.

Richard Bustillo

The basic training philosophy was that we were all preparing for a fight. A few fought in combat sports, but the main emphasis was training to win a street fight. It wasn't about exploring different martial arts for artistic expression, but was about enhancing our combat athleticism, working the basics hard, and testing it all in sparring.

Burt Richardson

Jeet kune do is part martial art, part rhetoric. Bruce Lee was a verbally dynamic person, and as good with words as he was with his hands and feet. Many of his personal moves worked for him because of his attributes, such as superb timing and speed, but they were not practical for others. In short, Bruce Lee could make ballet functional, and back up his arguments with demonstrations.

John Steven Soet

I would like to point out that to be a teacher is different than to be a practitioner. Bruce, as a teacher, had the ability to make you believe you could do it.

Bob Bremer

The largest single hurdle is simply to believe in or understand the concept. Once belief is achieved, what once was just a concept will become your best friend.

Paul Vunak

Bruce said, "Forget all that, we'll get to that. Right now, I'm trying to teach the *spirit* of what I'm talking about." That's what Bruce taught: the spirit of combat.

Stirling Silliphant

I felt there was some kenpo karate in many of his techniques. I never discussed this with him, but I would say that he had taken what he found useful from many arts and synthesized them into what worked best for him.

Joe Hyams

Bruce's statement that, "My truth is not your truth," doesn't mean that each one of us will all have totally different truths. I think it deals more with the philosophical premise that truth cannot be given to you.

Chris Kent

Because the truth is always relative to certain situations, his basic principle as a teacher was to help the student to find his own version of the truth. This philosophy of personal liberation led me to new discoveries in the martial arts.

Dan Inosanto

When people say Lee didn't learn the complete wing chun system, I agree with them in the classical sense, even though in the functional sense they're not entirely correct. How much does one really need to learn to truly understand what they have?

Robert Chu

JKD is the same, but the JKD scene and the martial art scene is not the same as in 1972. With arts like shoot-fighting, sport jiu-jitsu, MMA and Thai boxing, the American martial arts scene is very different than at Bruce Lee's time.

Cass Magda

Bruce had a training schedule and a training plan for the classes, but I don't think he ever followed it religiously, step by step. He improvised a lot according to the evolution of the class.

Pete Jacobs

The pursuit of perfection in all aspects of martial arts is not a bad thing and that is what we are attempting.

Taky Kimura

Bruce was very concerned about the moral character. He looked for a willingness to train, respect for him, and sincerity. He spent a lot of time developing his art so he didn't want to pass it on to people of dubious character.

Dan Lee

The art of JKD provides the freedom to not be bound by any technique— including the fundamentals if necessary—and to evolve and grow in your own process of existence.

Tim Tackett

We can use the fundamental structure developed by Bruce based on simplicity and directness to find a way to express ourselves in combat and in life as well.

Ted Wong

It's not easy to define Jeet Kune Do, but I would say that it's a blend of modern training methods and approaches with some very traditional theories.

Ted Lucaylucay

I once asked Bruce's permission if I could use one energy drill in kenpo. He wrote me a note, saying "A garden of roses will yield roses, a garden of violets will yield violets." This is what Bruce thought about mixing styles. It's crystal clear, isn't it?

Jerry Poteet

Bruce always emphasized that each person must research his own truth. Although one can copy the style of Rembrandt, one will not become Rembrandt.

Larry Hartsell

Because of my boxing background I was always on the balls of my feet. When I was studying kajukenbo the instructors kept telling me to be flat-footed. I couldn't! Sometimes you have to break tradition and question a few things in order to find yourself.

Richard Bustillo

If Bruce hadn't come along, I would have probably dropped out of martial arts because I was learning some stuff I didn't consider really useful.

Bob Bremer

I don't believe there should be a division between self-perfection and self-preservation. You don't see basketball players spending a lot of time on fancy movements that would be ineffective in actual game situations. I believe in self-perfection *through* the practice of self-preservation.

Burt Richardson

The underlying philosophy of JKD is continuous improvement through experimentation. It also means no single individual has it all, as Bruce himself didn't have it all at the time of his death.

John Steven Soet

JKD is not eclectic. Eclectic means to pick and choose from different systems or doctrines. Bruce Lee never picked anything! He discovered common flaws and hacked away at the unessential until his truth remained.

Paul Vunak

One of the things is that as an instructor, you're always working on ways to allow students to experience something without boxing them in.

Chris Kent

Whatever comes out of that process of finding their personal expression is the student's personal truth. It's not mine and it's not Bruce's.

Dan Inosanto

JKD is a process of liberation, not an end. Once you are liberated, you still have to do what you were doing before. Like the Zen saying, "Before enlightenment chop wood, carry water; After enlightenment chop wood, carry water."

Cass Magda

Bruce used to say to me: "Whenever some big guy attacks you, instead of reacting to *his* ego, teach him to react to yours."

Stirling Silliphant

I realized finally what one of the goals is in martial arts: acting without thought, without mind, without planning, I only reached that awareness years later and the breakthrough came while I was studying wing chun kung fu.

Joe Hyams

In my opinion, JKD is philosophy in action. Like yin/yang, the physical and the philosophical elements are two halves of a unified whole. You can't have one without the other.

Chris Kent

"That's not the way to bring out the art, Dan," he said to me. His system was never made for mass distribution.

Dan Inosanto

Everyone these days is "using what works." New eclectic styles preaching "totally" and "freedom of expression" are sprouting up everywhere.

Cass Magda

Bruce exchanged information with some top people and taught some others, but I guess what he really wanted to know was if he could convey what he was doing so others could make it work. And if not, should he modify or change it? We were his guinea pigs in a certain way.

Pete Jacobs

The idea is to use the arts to transcend our- selves by letting our spirit come through. That is the reason why I always believed and related martial arts discipline to mental discipline.

Taky Kimura

Bruce told me that being too comfortable with something was to my detriment. I was unaware of this, but he could touch me at will because he knew my rhythm and could fit in with it.

Dan Lee

Bruce didn't need to use anything other than a finger jab. That's what a JKD man looks for; to get something so well, so good, that that's all you need.

Tim Tackett

To Bruce, the totality of direct hand-to-hand combat meant all the possible approaches to combat. It *did not* and *does not* mean the sum of all the techniques of every "style" of martial arts ever invented. Totality is not the amalgamation of 16 or 32 or even 128 different martial arts systems.

Ted Wong

Jun Fan JKD is based on training yourself to be able to fight very effectively in the street environment where there are virtually no rules. Not just learning the techniques and theories, but actually engaging in the type of training that prepares you to fight well.

Burt Richardson

Jeet Kune Do has become JKD Lite, stalled at the beginning physical stage. Bruce was peeking beyond the veil of the physical world.

Jerry Poteet

JKD is more than just a method that borrows techniques from different styles.

Ted Lucaylucay

Bruce always talked about prostituting the art. And that's what's going on, under many disguises. That's why I can say with a clear conscience that I never taught Jeet Kune Do.

Leo T. Fong

Vince Lombardi once said, "When all else is equal, strength will tell." Physical conditioning is a very important factor in combat.

Larry Hartsell

It takes a lot of time and understanding to become an instructor and unfortunately alot of people can't invest that much.

Richard Bustillo

Sometimes we used to go to parties or celebrations and Bruce would sit around saying nothing because he had nothing to talk about but martial arts. In the meantime, everybody else was having fun!

Bob Bremer

Although Bruce Lee may not have been a master in the traditional Chinese sense, he is still deserving of high praise – not for being the founder of a martial art, a movie star, an early pioneer of wing chun in America, or even a role model for Chinese people everywhere, but rather for making his wing chun come alive.

Robert Chu

One must absorb what is useful and reject what is useless. How does one reject what is ultimately useless without applying it over and over again to find out its merits and faults.

Paul Vunak

The ultimate in combat, Bruce maintained, is to hit your opponent without being hit yourself.

Stirling Silliphant

There is a philosophy or an attitude one must use to look at the training and the art, but all those concepts are very universal and you can find them in many other styles besides JKD.

Ted Wong

As in athletics, to comprehend what a martial artist does, to appreciate how he pursues his art, you must understand the art. You must speak the language. And the martial artist should communicate effectively in his chosen medium of expression. That is why jeet kune do has remained so long a mystery to so many languages. It is a strangely complex and mystifying animal.

Tim Tackett

The fact of the matter is, Bruce never had a chosen successor. This is evidence by the fact that both Dan and Taky were older than Bruce. He hadn't planned on dying early, before he could crystallize his organization into something more cohesive. And when he did pass away, a problem was created by the personalities of the most well-versed practitioners–both Dan and Taky are modest men.

John Steven Soet

During Bruce's time grappling was not that strong. But Bruce looked at grappling from a different perspective than people today.

Bob Bremer

Bruce was right. My training had brought me to the point of *mushin*, meaning "no mind," or "it," as Bruce had said.

Joe Hyams

There are three main requirements. The first is that you've got to know yourself inside out. The second is that you've got to have a strong technical foundation in whatever you do, that should be continuously refined and upgraded or improved. And the third thing is that you've got to take whatever you do, integrate it with your personality, and add your own personal modifications to "make it your own.

Chris Kent

Bruce advocated the philosophy of "finding the cause of your own ignorance." He didn't like anything organized because according to him, "JKD does not have a blueprint."

Dan Inosanto

The philosophy of JKD is like any other philosophy, people can add or express their own interpretation of it. What Bruce Lee meant by the JKD philosophy in practical application is sometimes a far cry from those martial artists claiming to follow it.

Cass Magda

Bruce's forte was one-on-one teaching. I was only there for about a year but I haven't forgotten what he taught me.

Pete Jacobs

I have always found that martial arts discipline has always put me through psychological changes, and I honestly believe that anything that puts you up against yourself is going to be beneficial because you'll be more aware of who you are and, eventually, you'll transcend yourself.

Taky Kimura

For Bruce, the martial artist's tool was his punches and kicks, so you had to learn how to hit at any angle, with any rhythm, at any time.

Dan Lee

I really believe that JKD provides a way for everybody to create their own path—and not to just follow another's.

Tim Tackett

Jeet kune do is not a classical style. Its purpose is not to segregate, conditioner restrict. It does not hold the practitioner in bondage to one partial aspect of combat. The totality of combat is conditionless and bondless, since combat is never fixed, and is changing from moment to moment.

Ted Wong

Bruce wanted us to develop the physical tools of JKD until they were "masterpieces."

Jerry Poteet

In a commercial studio you can't go full blast all the time; the sparring has to be controlled and the way of teaching has to change. I was saying that a long time ago and I was heavily criticized for thinking this way.

Ted Lucaylucay

The Gracie Family proved the grappling arts are necessary and very efficient if you know how to use them. We have to give them a lot of credit for bringing grappling back to the public eye.

Larry Hartsell

Neither Dan Inosanto nor I wanted to capitalize on Bruce's name. There is no such thing as a JKD school as such.

Richard Bustillo

Bruce understood that in order to make an art unique, it must have a philosophical foundation.

Dan Lee

He left a framework to look at and if everybody had that first, they would become much better martial artists because they would be able to sort out what's effective and what's not, in a real situation.

Bob Bremer

The problem I found with many (definitely not all) of the JKD Concepts teachers is that while they have open minds and an open approach but stray far from the foundational JKD principle of pressure testing. Pressure testing is what allows each individual to determine what works for him or her.

Burt Richardson

The whole idea behind what Bruce was doing is not the accumulation of styles or techniques. Bruce didn't look at his art from a style perspective.

Pete Jacobs

According to Bruce's writings, "JKD has a tight structure in defense in attack." So why are some people adding to the JKD core entry techniques with the groin wide open?

Tim Tackett

The stop-hit is a concept Bruce Lee borrowed from fencing. It's really quite simple to understand; all that is involved is picking up any telegraphic moment on the part of your opponent and negating the attack with a strike of your own. It definitely calls for a high level of awareness and razor-sharp tools, but it is probably the most efficient way to inflict pain prior to an entry.

Paul Vunak

Bruce helped me realize the existence and importance of the 360-degree attack sector. On the other hand, one of the things that helped me in the transition was the fact that, through fencing, my reflexes had been tuned to accommodate blindingly fast counter- attacks.

Stirling Silliphant

Bruce had honed his mind with the study of Zen which played a strong role in his spiritual approach to Jeet Kune Do.

Joe Hyams

The people who were actually there and training in the art under Dan never used the name Jeet Kune Do in a commercial way. It was kind of like an unwritten code. You didn't capitalize on the name.

Chris Kent

I think martial arts is an enjoyable thing to do while you're living here on this earth. It's a great vehicle which helps you to grow by allowing you to know other people and also yourself.

Dan Inosanto

Dan Inosanto had this certain perspective on things. He was fun to be with. I remember him especially being like a little kid when it came to learning new things.

Cass Magda

My view of the very essence of what Bruce was trying to teach is to help us to find our own way of looking—not only at martial arts but also life.

Pete Jacobs

The realistic approach to fighting that he used later on to create the art of Jeet Kune Do was taking form within him because he already had what he felt was the most useful from all these styles.

Taky Kimura

I want to develop JKD techniques that will live up to Bruce's expectations as depicted in his JKD emblem and philosophy.

Dan Lee

Technique wise at Dan's backyard, we drilled JKD basics such as the straight punch, and footwork. We used different equipment like focus gloves, kicking shields, and heavy bags. We worked on trying to intercept the opponent's action from the very beginning, which is the very essence of Jeet Kune Do.

Tim Tackett

Bruce changed the delivery system of the technique and not the technique in itself. He was evolving in a certain direction, not jumping from system to system.

Ted Wong

Bruce was a perfectionist and things were done his way or no way. The sessions were very demanding.

Jerry Poteet

If you have the guts to go to the highest level, then break free of Bruce Lee and his JKD. Because that's JKD's greatest test—to evolve to the point where you don't allow anyone or any philosophy to dictate your life.

Ted Lucaylucay

Bruce changed my whole perception about fighting. He added mobility and a lot of footwork. That basic concept modified many things.

Larry Hartsell

I think that the best way to describe the basic idea of JKD is to use the analogy of writing. I can teach a class how to write in cursive, but pretty soon every student will come out with his own personal penmanship—a penmanship that only each particular writer can produce.

Richard Bustillo

It is not just *knowing* the core techniques, but training in them until you can efficiently use them and know how and why they work for you.

Bob Bremer

Sticking only to what Bruce Lee did was actually against his philosophy. Just look at what his symbol says: "Using no way as way, having no limitation as limitation." It doesn't say, "Only using Bruce Lee's way, and limiting yourself to what Bruce Lee did."

Burt Richardson

Perhaps the biggest mistake students make is to try to recreate what Bruce Lee did by Thai boxing, doing a little Wing Chun here and there, and so on. Though their hearts are in the right places, the focus is all wrong.

Paul Vunak

Bruce wrote, "If you understand motion, you don't need style." That means being free of styles or even combinations of styles.

Chris Kent

A JKD man has to look and explore these methods to see what can be absorbed in order to make what he has better.

Dan Inosanto

Bruce would say, "What is the simplest and fastest way to kick from here with my lead leg?" This would lead him to develop a way of kicking—and that kick might resemble a Savate technique, a northern shaolin technique, or something else.

Pete Jacobs

If you don't really understand JKD principles and techniques, you can't add according to what is JKD.

Tim Tackett

Knowledge has no understanding. Understanding comes from your own individual experiences with that knowledge.

Cass Magda

One of the problems Bruce faced in teaching me; to try to get me to initiate attacks. He finally perceived that it just wasn't my nature and instead he drilled me on counterattacks, at which, in fencing, if I say so myself, I was one tricky, high-scoring fighter.

Stirling Silliphant

Self-defense is not why I started to study the martial arts in the first place. Self-defense ability was only an accidental byproduct, just as Zen was an accidental by-product of my studies.

Joe Hyams

Dan has excellent organizational and presentation skills. He's also a master teacher. I've seen him teach something five different ways to reach different kinds of people.

Chris Kent

I was liberated as a martial artist because after learning from him I didn't feel trapped or caught in any style. I am free to train, research and develop myself in the way I want to.

Dan Inosanto

Inosanto could be very critical in private about the functionality of certain things. He had great research methods and learning techniques. That was valuable to me.

Cass Magda

I don't like to advise people, but the most important thing is to be honest with yourself. In reality, if you're not honest to yourself everything you do in life will be a lie.

Pete Jacobs

I understand that the traditional teachers do not teach 100 percent, but that they keep things for themselves in case some student turns on them.

Taky Kimura

I would recommend reading Bruce's own writing in the way of Jeet Kune Do. Try to follow Bruce's guidelines in order to develop your full potential through diligent training and practice using the yin/yang philosophy.

Dan Lee

The name of the school was The Jun Fan Gung Fu Institute, but the art of JKD was never named "Jun Fan gung fu" until Bruce Lee passed away.

Tim Tackett

Remember, "change" doesn't mean learning ten different ways of punching every month. It also doesn't mean to change from one style to another after a year, or anything remotely like that.

Ted Wong

Bruce said you needed to "step through the door of insanity" and be able to come back. That's why moral character was so important to him.

Jerry Poteet

Get a good foundation in JKD and then be open- minded enough to develop your own way of doing things. After you understand the basis, the vehicle is not that important because the JKD principles intertwine.

Ted Lucaylucay

There was a lot physical conditioning. Because Bruce's interest was in working with the individual, he kept the classes very small.

Larry Hartsell

To the unknowledgeable observer JKD may only appear to be various separate elements such as boxing, wrestling, wing chun, loosely strong together to create one generalized martial art. But that is an illusion, and to embrace the illusion is to invite defeat.

Tim Tackett

Unfortunately, people today seem to put money first by selling contracts, certifications, instructorship ranks, and trying to use the Jeet Kune Do name strictly for personal gain.

Richard Bustillo

Bruce Lee was above all else concerned with function. His entire martial art was built around functionality, reality, and totality. JKD is based upon street-fighting, without any rules or regulations and in which anything goes.

Chris Kent

What is exciting and vital about JKD to me is that it is a format for the individual to grow and become. You don't stop researching or learning because you think the founder did it all and knows it all.

Cass Magda

The added problem faced by JKD practitioners is that many seek to become attached to the legacy of Bruce Lee not out of love of the art or the desire to improve one's skills, but out of the desire to be linked on a third-generation basis to a major film star. JKD is not an art. It's a harmonic, yet deadly, blend of many things, most of which are not applicable in the ring.

Paul Vunak

Unfortunately, I see many people adding things without having a deep understanding of how the JKD core techniques work in combat.

Bob Bremer

I think that's exactly what the JKD idea is. All of us learned to write the letters of the alphabet by following a model in a textbook of how each letter should look. But none of us write the letters exactly like the template because we are all different. Each individual in JKD *should* have a different approach. You should end up doing, as Sifu Richard Bustillo would say often, "your own JKD".

Burt Richardson

Bruce wanted to make the cost of each lesson so prohibitive that if anybody took it, he would damn well concentrate on the business at hand.

Stirling Silliphant

To "express yourself" is to give expression to your feelings, emotions, and imagination in whatever you do.

Chris Kent

Bruce picked up things from a lot of people and I felt honored to share the knowledge that I had of other systems and styles.

Dan Inosanto

In order to go beyond the physical, you need something else and Bruce used the philosophical approach to transcend the technical and physical levels.

Pete Jacobs

The idea of absorbing what is useful does not mean choosing, collecting, compiling, accumulating or assembling techniques from different styles of martial arts thinking to yourself. "I'll take the best from all the styles and put it together to form a new style."

Cass Magda

I don't think I can ever pay Bruce back for what he did for me as a friend. So I do my best to keep his memory alive.

Taky Kimura

Bruce's philosophy was efficiency at all costs and to become a good fighter you must spar with other good fighters—just as to become a good swimmer you must swim in the water and not on land.

Dan Lee

I look at Bruce Lee as a well-rounded human being; he was martial artist, teacher, writer, actor, philosopher, father, and husband. He was also one of the first martial art "human potential" proselytizers.

Chris Kent

The problem is that many people think that they are capable of expressing themselves when they really don't understand what Jeet Kune Do is all about.

Tim Tackett

I ask that all JKD practitioners bind together for the sake of the future of jeet kune do and for the memory of Bruce Lee. We are only as strong as our weakest link. The key to group cohesion is communication, clarification, and understanding.

Ted Wong

JKD has struggled from a backyard system to a public system. It basically developed without a plan. "To be known by many and practiced by few" was the motto back then.

Cass Magda

The problem is that students are only getting the physical curriculum. In order for combat to be a martial art, it needs a philosophical foundation. Otherwise, you are just accumulating techniques.

Jerry Poteet

JKD has to be versatile for all ages whether they look for exercise, self-defense or to release stress. We have to understand the value of the reward system and even if we didn't give belts, I felt that we needed to offer something to give the students some recognition and prestige.

Ted Lucaylucay

Any range can be closed very quickly, so you need to know how to adapt. Sometimes grappling is not a good idea.

Larry Hartsell

The martial arts have evolved during the last twenty years, so the JKD practitioner needs to understand this evolution and adapt his method to efficiently deal with them.

Richard Bustillo

You need practice. It's just like a pilot, the more hours you fly makes you a better pilot—and the more hours you spar makes you a better fighter.

Bob Bremer

All I do is martial arts. I spend hours each day training, studying, pondering, and on some days, teaching. I train and study much more than I teach. That allows me the luxury of going very deep into various arts, continuing to study and improve long after I have become considered (by my instructors) an expert in a particular art.

Burt Richardson

Why don't JKD people compete? They were competing full contact before there was full contact, Bruce trained an aide corps of intense streetfighters full contact before the sport was ever invented.

Paul Vunak

He charged so much to place value on his instruction and make himself stand out as someone very, very different. This is an Asian attitude, a way of showing that the lesson offered has worth—the fee is merely the token of this, not the point of it.

Stirling Silliphant

If everyone thought and actualized themselves like Bruce Lee, then JKD schools really wouldn't be necessary.

Chris Kent

Bruce had a personal, base system. He said that you had to capture the essence of each art. The essence is not the three-thousand techniques you have to learn from white belt to black belt.

Dan Inosanto

To "absorb" means to "get into" the technique, training method and art you are interested in until you develop a "feel" for it. Until you experience "being" in it and becoming it you don't really understand it.

Cass Magda

Bruce realized that in order to reach the very nature of the student he had to explain things in a different context, with a philosophical approach.

Pete Jacobs

I kept the school out of respect for Bruce. It's a private club. I don't feel the need to be in the public eye and I really enjoy sharing with a small group of people what I learned from Bruce.

Taky Kimura

Bruce told me once: "Dan, open your mind and do your own thinking and research." This has been my philosophy in life.

Dan Lee

There is a level in JKD where you can't teach the student anymore. This is because JKD's highest level is about personal expression in combat.

Tim Tackett

In sparring in JKD, the student wears full protective equipment and goes all out; in this way, he can truly learn the correct timing and distance for punches and kick and become immediately familiar with what it is like to fight under these conditions.

Ted Wong

It bothers me the utter commercialization of Bruce's art. And you can't get around it by calling it "original Jeet Kune Do," or "JKD concepts."

Jerry Poteet

They said, "You can't teach JKD to the masses," but these same individuals were teaching big seminar groups on the weekend.

Ted Lucaylucay

Even if grappling is not your strong point, you'd better know how to deal with it. In order to efficiently deal with something, you'd better know it and understand it first. You have to learn how to deal with grappling.

Larry Hartsell

As far as the base system concerns, we are the same, but our understanding of the principles of Jeet Kune Do may take us to a different expression.

Richard Bustillo

The cool thing is that when people of equal, or even different levels of understanding get involved in a live discussion, new insights can emerge that might never have seen the light of day without the exchange.

Chris Kent

A point should be made about the term "modified." Modifications were never made just for the sake of change, or simply because something looked pretty or better. Modification is how Jun Fan evolved gradually, through a constant process of trial and error, and experimentation. A technique was modified only because it did not theoretically accomplish what Bruce felt it should, and nothing was changed unless a genuine improvement could be demonstrated.

Tim Tackett

We can add a technique if it fits the criteria of simplicity and directness and fits our structure. We also add our own attitude and our own personality. We add our own unique point of view or philosophy of fighting.

Cass Magda

A lot of people tend to skip understanding and interpreting Bruce's notes and jump right to evaluation, deciding whether something is right or wrong before they really understand what it says or means.

Chris Kent

The way of JKD is motion through life. It is the doing and not what is done, the journey and not the destination, and the experience and not the outcome.

Paul Vunak

Training realistically was the whole idea behind his teaching—being able to use what you have in a real fight. Because we sparred a lot, we could see our progress and judge how well we were doing.

Bob Bremer

I realized through combat sports that it wasn't my technique that was lacking, but rather my method of practicing. I was not doing enough sparring to develop the ability to read an opponent and to properly time my attacks or counterattacks.

Burt Richardson

A lot of people have misunderstood Dan Inosanto's personal evolution as a martial artist and confused it with their own practicing or teaching of JKD.

Chris Kent

Bruce gave me the building blocks and the inquiring mind to develop myself as a martial artist. He gave the functional eye to look at things from a practical perspective and see what works under what kind of circumstances.

Dan Inosanto

I am surprised even today that I'll do something or come up with something really cool and I'll hear Dan Inosanto in my brain say, "That's good, but it's always been there; you're just rediscovering it, so don't get a swelled head."

Cass Magda

The JKD physical foundation is a great beginning. But don't forget that in your personal evolution, just because you "think" that something is JKD, it doesn't make it JKD.

Pete Jacobs

Bruce didn't care what race or nationality you were either. That attitude brought him some problems because some Chinese masters felt uncomfortable with him teaching non-Chinese people.

Taky Kimura

Interception is just one aspect of the whole art. It may be the highest level of defense because you stop the attack before it begins.

Ted Wong

Dan Inosanto promised Bruce Lee to never commercialize the art. Later on, Inosanto opened the old Kali Academy in Torrance, California. He was into the Filipino arts and he didn't want to push Jeet Kune Do too openly so he began to call it Jun Fan gung fu.

Tim Tackett

The essence of JKD is simplicity, the stripping down of all the non-essentials.

Dan Lee

I wanted to accelerate my progress, so I asked Bruce what I should do. He said, "I'll have something for you at the next training session." And he did. Bruce gave me a personalized training program to do at home every day.

Jerry Poteet

I believe that the philosophy of totality in JKD is about the free acceptance of all martial arts. It's not exclusive, but inclusive.

Ted Lucaylucay

Bruce emphasized understanding timing and rhythm, and he always maintained that it was better to have five or six techniques that you can really use rather than 200 techniques that you just know.

Larry Hartsell

Some people used to assist in seminars, receive their seminar certificate, which was just an hours-trained certification, and then go open a JKD school! It was unbelievable. A seminar certificate is not an instructor's certificate.

Richard Bustillo

I really believe that you need the foundation of what Bruce was teaching back then because it is your base for further growth and evolution.

Bob Bremer

I think a big reason that many schools avoid sparring is because people mistake sparring with fighting. Very few people want to go to a class they're paying for to get beaten up. That is destructive. We need to understand that sparring and fighting are quite different.

Burt Richardson

The scope of JKD's is not a style, but is art. Actually, it is the artistic process of more fully realizing our potential and expressing a way of life.

Paul Vunak

It's okay if you like this art or that art, but that doesn't mean that because you're doing it, you're doing Jeet Kune Do.

Chris Kent

You can find some JKD principles in Thai boxing, savate, kali, et cetera, and use the JKD approach or mentality to work with the technical material of these arts—and that's OK—but it doesn't automatically make these other arts JKD.

Dan Inosanto

I think the most important thing Dan Inosanto taught me was to just love martial arts with every part of your being and soul.

Cass Magda

We all found our way of doing what Bruce was teaching and because the material he was sharing was based on simplicity and a natural way of moving the body, the only way we can truly make it work is teaching in our personal mold.

Pete Jacobs

He was talking about "liberating" the martial artist when a lot of people didn't understand what it means "to be a slave of a style."

Taky Kimura

Bruce said, "The height of cultivation runs into simplicity, the ability to express the utmost with the minimum. It is the halfway cultivation that leads to ornamentation."

Dan Lee

If you look at his philosophical notes, Bruce was greatly influenced by Taoism, Zen, and Jiddu Krishnamurti but, interestingly enough, he was heavily influenced by Western philosophy also—which gave him pragmatism and the scientific method at the same time.

Tim Tackett

The teacher should teach Bruce's core system and help and assist the student in developing his own way once this core has been properly mastered. Otherwise, everybody will be doing something different and call it Jeet Kune Do.

Ted Wong

A martial art is much more than the physical, and after all, punching, kicking and grappling is only beginning-level martial art

Jerry Poteet

Bruce used to say that you owe allegiance only to yourself. So you had to be free from any martial arts style or system.

Larry Hartsell

If a person is saying that they've evolved or developed themselves to Bruce Lee's level or beyond, either physically or mentally, that's one thing. But to say that you've evolved the art of Jeet Kune Do, which is based on totality, reality, and functionality, is quite another thing.

Chris Kent

I don't think liberation can come to every JKD practitioner any more than *satori* can come to everyone studying Zen or *nirvana* to every Hindu. Just because we practice JKD doesn't mean we are liberated.

Cass Magda

I'm not getting into all the hype of the "original JKD" or "JKD concepts" thing. What some JKD people are trying to do is just sell their politics. And I don't have time for that.

Ted Lucaylucay

We look at combat not as a sport but as total fighting, and many aspects probably don't fit into the sport aspect. But we do like to go and get the ring and competition experience depending on the student's wishes and motivation.

Richard Bustillo

Just remember that Bruce used to say, "It's not what you can learn, it's what you can throw away." That means going back to simplicity. That was his whole thing—simplicity!

Bob Bremer

We start sparring very light and add tools and intensity over time. I borrowed a term from body building and call it "progressive resistance". Nobody has to spar hard ever. That is a personal choice. Just keep in mind that while sparring hard is more dangerous, it also gives us more realistic feedback.

Burt Richardson

When a fighter always uses the same rhythm, he establishes "routine" which is a type of telegraphing and leaves him more susceptible to his opponent's counters, stop-hits, and broken rhythms. He leaves himself open to be read, like so many pages in a book.

Paul Vunak

To me, there are JKD practitioners and there are martial art practitioners who are using some JKD principles or concepts in their training. They're not the same thing.

Chris Kent

I do use the principles of JKD to work with any particular system but that's a personal ability developed by the understanding of the JKD philosophy. I might express some JKD principles using kali techniques, but when I'm teaching kali I don't say that I'm teaching JKD.

Dan Inosanto

I can compare the art of Jeet Kune Do to a beautiful, sculptured object. The final product is awesome but how did he do it?

Taky Kimura

Let's say that I teach the JKD principles behind the five ways of attack, but I explain how these principles are applied using kali techniques or pentjak silat movements. The techniques I'm teaching are not from Jeet Kune Do but the way of explaining the principles behind these techniques are coming from JKD.

Cass Magda

The essence is that if you want to do something, do it—but do it for yourself and not for anyone else. And if it happens that you fall, you fall down on your own terms. In the end I believe the greatest reward is to be honest with yourself.

Pete Jacobs

Our training should never be bound by a style or system. Dare to set yourself free to experiment with different ways to use your techniques.

Dan Lee

Because the name "Jeet Kune Do" was directly related to Bruce Lee and neither one of us wanted to capitalize on Bruce's name to promote ourselves or the art.

Tim Tackett

Bruce wanted to give a simple and effective way of looking at the things while still having the individual as the most relevant factor in the equation.

Ted Wong

Bruce was trying to teach us the difference between "doing" and "being." In other words, don't just do the movement, be the movement.

Jerry Poteet

In order to break the rules, you should know them. And many people are discarding things just because Bruce dropped them in his later years, without realizing that Bruce "had them" before he dropped them.

Ted Lucaylucay

Bruce always emphasized "His truth was not our truth." His whole JKD philosophy was meant to be a process of self-discovery and problem solving.

Larry Hartsell

Personally, I like to teach everything; I don't hold anything back. I'm not doing my job unless my students can eventually kick my butt!"

Richard Bustillo

Probably, that lack of understanding is the reason so many are adding so much to JKD these days.

Bob Bremer

In my eyes, if an instructor candidate cannot spar well, then he or she doesn't have a deep understanding of how to apply the art, they shouldn't teach until they are competent in sparring.

Burt Richardson

At a high level, you can't teach JKD because in a way it's an experience—an idea for personal expression.

Dan Inosanto

The "JKD Concepts" name became an umbrella term to practice four or five different styles and relate them to Jeet Kune Do for commercial purposes.

Tim Tackett

Every time we compare "this JKD man" to "that JKD man" or this school to that school or this article to that article, etc. we are blindly searching for "the one Way," which defeats the whole purpose. We have to free ourselves from the priorities of "best and worst" and "right and wrong."

Paul Vunak

A boxer can use some of the principles and concepts that are in JKD, but if he stays only in Western boxing and never goes out of that realm, he is still partialized, and therefore not doing JKD.

Chris Kent

Bruce talked about his new style being a combination of fencing, boxing, and wing chun as the central core. I think that explanation changed as he got into Krishnamurti and others and tried to make his method have no boundaries and no identifiable elements.

Cass Magda

Efficiency means getting out as much as you put in. You have to make sure that you hit what you are after. Technique by itself doesn't give you efficiency.

Pete Jacobs

Unfortunately, I have seen the effects of exploitation and inadequacy in Jeet Kune Do and rarely, if ever, do many gain more than just a physical under- standing of what the art is all about.

Taky Kimura

I think that the term "Jeet Kune Do" itself does not convey the total meaning of the art. Bruce always reminded us to constantly research on our own.

Dan Lee

After reaching a certain point you should work really hard to maintain your level of physical condition as high as you can.

Ted Wong

The evolution he talked about is on a personal, individual level. Jeet Kune Do is the key that brings about that change and evolution.

Jerry Poteet

We don't reject anything until we know why we're doing it. We could be throwing away something really great because of our own lack of understanding or our lack of ability in timing, or distance.

Cass Magda

Bruce's writings and notes make his positions very clear with regard to his own personal development as a martial artist and the application of his philosophy to his way of living.

Chris Kent

The JKD liberation comes from learning to appreciate all the martial arts styles and not by disassociating yourself from all the traditional root.

Ted Lucaylucay

You can't teach or train Joe Frazier the same way you train Muhammad Ali. I really believe that you can only guide the student to find the cause of his own ignorance.

Larry Hartsell

Nowadays, circumstances have changed. Of course we do spar, but the mentality is different. We drill much more than before.

Richard Bustillo

Our JKD usable knowledge has increased. It's good to look at different arts but you must be careful what you add.

Bob Bremer

I also believe that a JKD-labeled practitioner should not be limited to those who only practice what Bruce Lee did in his tragically short lifetime. Start with Jun Fan JKD as a base, and as you expand, be sure that the principle of street-specific pressure testing remains front and center.

Burt Richardson

Perhaps the only criteria of an "authentic" JKD spokesperson rests with his fighting skills, technical prowess, or duration of study. It is, however, important to measure duration of study in terms of hours, not years.

Paul Vunak

To me, there's nothing wrong with investigating other arts, just make sure you know why you are investigating them and what you hope to get out of it.

Chris Kent

He began to apply the philosophical principles and concepts he used to develop JKD to other aspects of his life. The JKD principles are interchangeable with other endeavors because it's a problem-solving philosophy that teaches you how to find what works for your- self at any given time or place, both in combat and in life.

Dan Inosanto

I think Bruce wanted to find a way to talk about JKD where he didn't have to label it as any one thing or be compared to any one thing.

Cass Magda

In the end it is not about what kind of technique you do but how skillful you are using it, and your timing and rhythm to place it in the right spot at the right time.

Pete Jacobs

Bruce was very perceptive as a teacher because he knew that I was only capable of assimilating a certain amount of knowledge at any given point, so he never threw a bunch of stuff at me.

Taky Kimura

In my classes, I am able not just to talk about fighting, but to help people to understand the principle of yin/yang and apply it to their lives.

Dan Lee

You may train in jiu-jitsu, Thai boxing and pull out a few things because of the JKD principles—but they are still jiu-jitsu and Thai boxing, not JKD.

Tim Tackett

Only after mastering footwork and distance can you really use the technique—the third element—according to the JKD framework.

Ted Wong

"Add what is specifically your own." People justify whatever they are doing as JKD, no matter how far afield it is from Bruce's art, because they don't understand that expression.

Jerry Poteet

We were doing wing chun trapping and Western boxing instead of a karate punch or a kung-fu crescent kick because we had "some- thing better" and we were "liberated." Let me tell you, we were missing the point.

Ted Lucaylucay

Bruce always said that a good teacher was "A pointer of the truth, not a giver of the truth." So you have to learn and grow to your own truths through your own abilities and understanding.

Larry Hartsell

The art has expanded, and the teachers are much more open to everybody. Back then, Jeet Kune Do was very closed-door. We were very secretive, we didn't like to expose things.

Richard Bustillo

The "added stuff" that I see these days made me realize just how good the stuff that Bruce taught us at the Chinatown school really was.

Bob Bremer

Jeet Kune Do must remain alive. Each individual practitioner must become a competent fighter, through fighting, instead of a master of memorization. Real fighting is about relating to an opponent in the moment.

Burt Richardson

Jeet Kune Do was designed for a purpose— to intercept. I like to think of JKD as a speedboat with a 600-horsepower engine.

Cass Magda

How long are we going to waste our time on semantics. Why don't we just be thankful for what we've been given?

Paul Vunak

In 100 years, we're all going to be worm food. We might have some seventy or eighty years, that's some 23,000 days on this earth. Twenty-three thousand chances to "seize the day."

While JKD is built around combat and reality, it's not solely about fighting. To say JKD is "just about fighting" is like holding up a single grain of sand and saying, "This is the beach."

Chris Kent

To "absorb" means to "get into" the technique, or training method, or philosophy or whatever it is that you're interested in until you develop a "feel" for it. Until you experience "being and becoming" you don't really understand it. It's only then you can start to "reject what is useless."

Cass Magda

It isn't necessary for you to study every form of grappling. Hell, that would be impossible. What's important is that you understand and grasp the "essence" of grappling and have a good working knowledge of it so that if you find yourself in a grappling situation you know how to deal with it.

Chris Kent

After having the JKD foundation the practitioner can emphasize that aspect if he so chooses. If another guy prefers to stay outside, his personal research will develop that aspect. But both of them, as JKD men, have to understand the other aspects of combat.

Dan Inosanto

Bruce didn't mean *chi sao* was useless, but only that it was not the nucleus of what he was teaching in Los Angeles.

Taky Kimura

Bruce also emphasized mobility. Footwork was the very key of his art and he got information from Western fencing

Ted Wong

I look for a balance, for a yin/yang concept in my life and in my JKD.

Dan Lee

Today, the styles are much more open than before and usually adapt alot of things from other arts.

Tim Tackett

Once you control the physical movements at will it is not a "technique" anymore, it becomes a reflex and internal skill. And when you have that skill all you need to know is where to put it. Your body will "feel" it. If you can do that, you've got the game.

Pete Jacobs

I would be very skeptical to see someone surpass Bruce's genius. Let me see one original idea, let alone volumes of rich philosophy and a brilliant martial art. Bruce has already done the research for us.

Jerry Poteet

These days people teach for a living. Bruce said to my JKD peers not to commercialize JKD, but at a certain point in his life he was planning to open a chain of schools to teach the art.

Ted Lucaylucay

JKD is Bruce's art and having this as a base, I can find my personal martial art expression but not everybody has their own Jeet Kune Do as such.

Richard Bustillo

The JKD man has to be well-rounded in all JKD areas, but he needs to know his pluses and minuses as an individual.

Dan Inosanto

The JKD tree is going in many different ways. Some are seeking the original stuff, and that's good—but they have to question themselves if they are satisfied with it, because Bruce didn't mean for them to stop there.

Bob Bremer

For those who train in authentic Jun Fan JKD, where sparring is the most important training method, will eventually earn the right to have great confidence while remaining humble. Just as Bruce Lee found that a lot of his prejudices were wrong, we can discover the causes of our ignorance, change them, and become better people.

Burt Richardson

The bottom line is one must truly commit to living the way of JKD. This involves some fundamental principles such as relaxation, instinct, awareness, evasiveness, interception, emotional control, dissolving the ego, etc.

Paul Vunak

Totality in combat is the key. See the strengths in each particular element, but also see the potential weaknesses. Keep the big picture in mind. And don't lock yourself into thinking, "This is the only art."

Chris Kent

JKD is a racing boat. If you put six tons of cargo on it, it doesn't move fast anymore. It has to move very slowly so the cargo doesn't tip over. It's burdened by all the cargo you put on it.

Cass Magda

For Bruce the "secret" was in the body and not in fancy techniques or movements. The simplest and the more direct way is always the best.

Pete Jacobs

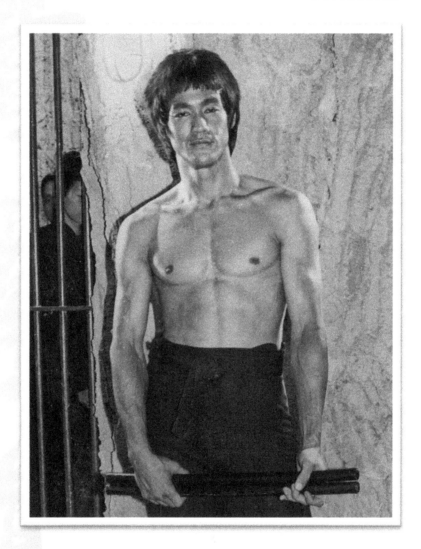

Bruce changed my way of thinking and looking at myself. He told me I'm just as good as anyone else and I began to believe in myself.

Taky Kimura

I think Tai Chi and JKD complement each other. Through the movements of tai chi I found the peace of mind and contentment that other martial arts failed to provide. Even in JKD combat, I have peace within myself.

Dan Lee

JKD is not a do-whatever-you-want approach. You can't just put a little bit of this and a little bit of that together and magically end up with JKD.

Tim Tackett

For Bruce physical condition was number one. If your body can't perform, then it doesn't matter how many techniques you know because you won't be able of use them in combat.

Ted Wong

If you look in the mirror, you might not like what you see at that moment. Then you have two choices. One is to change the view, and the other is to walk away and not look in the mirror anymore.

Chris Kent

I'll tell you something, if you accept only one dollar for teaching Jeet Kune Do you are commercializing the art—you are a commercial JKD instructor.

Ted Lucaylucay

Even though Bruce looked at everything, he didn't practice everything.

Bob Bremer

For small people, at first glance, the intelligent thing to do is to stay out of the reach of a bigger opponent. Unfortunately, you don't always get to choose the environment to fight, so you may not have that option.

Larry Hartsell

We can use the physical art he was teaching and take it as a base, educating the students to reach higher levels and eventually their own martial arts expression.

Richard Bustillo

For me personally, I think the ultimate goal of training realistically in the martial arts is to build confidence in yourself so that you can display kindness from strength to people you do not know. You don't have to be afraid to ask a stranger if they need help. You can smile at strangers regardless of what their reaction might be.

Burt Richardson

My advice to all students inquiring as to which art or arts to study is watch your potential instructor, but don't listen to his mouth, listen to his body.

Paul Vunak

The thing to keep foremost in mind is that JKD ultimately deals with relating to live, non-cooperating opponents, and in order to be able to do that you need to work out with other people.

Chris Kent

The important thing about rejecting what is useless is that you don't reject anything until you know why you are rejecting it.

Cass Magda

I never wanted to teach on a big scale—I'm not that kind of guy. Keeping my group small allows me to decide who I want and who I don't want to teach.

Pete Jacobs

You may fight many times and not learn anything from those experiences, and in the end, you won't have any direct experience to pass on.

Taky Kimura

Bruce once said: "Yin and yang are a pair of mutually complementary and interdependent forces that act continuously without cessation. Yin/Yang is one inseparable force on unceasing interplay of movement."

Dan Lee

Bruce was advocating that each student find the cause of their own ignorance, which does mean not going to your instructor for answers. To be able to walk alone, you need a high level of JKD philosophy understanding.

Dan Inosanto

You need the roots and you need the trunk—that's what Jeet Kune Do is for us.

Tim Tackett

I started teaching in order to keep learning and training. I needed someone to play with!

Pete Jacobs

The basic idea to become a good fighter is that you have to be trained to be a good fighter; and so to become a good teacher you have to be trained and taught to be a good teacher.

Taky Kimura

Some people say that what I'm teaching is very simple, but if you look at Bruce's notes and philosophy and compare them with what I'm doing—I'm very happy with what they're saying. I feel flattered because that's what JKD is all about—simplicity.

Ted Wong

Most of the time it's your own fault that the technique doesn't work, so before you reject anything make sure you've investigated why it doesn't work for you.

Cass Magda

If you research grappling you need a JKD grappling mentality, otherwise you'll be missing some important aspects.

Bob Bremer

The concept is that we cannot be the same. If you don't have the right level of understanding in JKD you may get lost in the process. That's why I say that JKD is a level of understanding, and I guess it is because if you really understand the physical art and the philosophy then you can become your own teacher.

Dan Inosanto

JKD is the art of expressing the human body, your body, in combat. It's a rational, well thought out approach to martial art training.

Chris Kent

Having all the technical requirements in the physical JKD curriculum doesn't assure you of being knowledgeable in JKD matters. That's why time is everything. You need time to mature as a JKD man. It gives you the perspective and maturity to use the philosophy not only for JKD, but for life itself.

Dan Inosanto

Bruce started with the principles and concepts as the bottom line—not a physical technique—and then developed something that could exemplify those principles. If you look at the way he moved, all his actions were very natural.

Pete Jacobs

In JKD we flow as in flowing from one aspect of fighting to another, such as punching to elbowing, but we don't mix styles to flow together.

Cass Magda

I'm not here to tell students that what we have is better than this style or that style. I'm just interested in being in my little corner.

Taky Kimura

Bruce applied the principles of softness and pliability to overcoming hardness, and the quality of water for adaptability to meet the changing situation.

Dan Lee

We use JKD as a base or a foundation—everything else has to fit onto that foundation. There are some good things that we use from other martial arts like Thai boxing, jiu-jitsu, or shoot wrestling—but we don't call them JKD—we call them Thai boxing, jiu-jitsu or shoot wrestling.

Tim Tackett

Be honest, would you? How can a person who has studied for 10 hours even hope to be qualified to teach JKD or any art for that matter? It's ridiculous.

Chris Kent

You can use the concepts or principles and apply them to other arts, but it doesn't make them JKD.

Ted Wong

Bruce knew that what he developed for himself it might not work as well for other people and that's the reason he said, "Add what is your own." He wanted you to find out what really worked for you as an individual.

Bob Bremer

A lot of the terminology used comes from "Inner Circle" conversations, so some terms mean something in particular at certain times. Some of these terms have been used openly in articles and seminars and were explained poorly and later on created a lot of confusion.

Cass Magda

TECHNIQUE

Lee was also fencing at this time and the efficiency and high-level tactics of fencing became imbued in Bruce Lee's approach. He discarded more of the Wing Chun approach and added the fencing principles of strong side forward, efficient footwork, various ways of attack, and other tactics. Jeet Kune Do was, as Bruce Lee called it, "fencing without a sword". Blend this with the upper body movement, curved punches, and circular footwork of boxing, add the kicks, and you have the foundation of Jun Fan JKD.

Burt Richardson

The idea is not to be a Lee clone, but a self-expressed martial artist. Done properly, this could only make a practitioner of any martial art superior. The problem is while JKD people decry traditionalism, this is exactly the philosophy of traditional martial arts.

John Steven Soet

When Lee created his Jun Fan kung fu, he was marketing a modified form of wing chun that he created, which bore his name. Many buy into the concept Jun Fan, but in truth it is neither jeet kune do nor wing chun.

Robert Chu

Bruce would demonstrate something like closing the gap, and then talk and lecture about it for half an hour. He didn't line us up and go 1-2-3 and drill us over and over like traditional schools. It was very "hang loose," very informal.

Leo T. Fong

There are just too many variables and too many scenarios when even the most talented fighter can find himself in a vulnerable position (i.e., mass attack, sucker punches, beer bottles over the head, just plain dumb luck, etc.) The simple fact is that most martial artists never put themselves in a position to test their mettle.

Paul Vunak

Bruce taught me his techniques of fighting, but the truth is I was not capable of using them. But he had been such a great teacher, was such a great master, that for the two or three years I studied with him I really believed I could do all these wonderful things he was showing me.

Stirling Silliphant

Bruce told me: "You have to come to me with an empty mind. You'll have to forget what you have learned previously."

Joe Hyams

Bruce said once that I needed to work on "my basic requirements." I didn't know what he meant so I asked him and he said, "You need to put some muscle on!"

Ted Wong

You have to remember that JKD is about totality, the whole pie. This includes kicking, punching, trapping, throwing, locking, et cetera.

Chris Kent

Personally, I don't want to focus on grappling, I want to focus on defending against grappling. But in order to do that, I need to understand grappling. So you need to learn how to grapple, but you don't have to be fixated on grappling if you can train to avoid it.

Tim Tackett

During his last visit, we went to the backyard gym at my house where he caught me up on some of his latest discoveries. This was the last time I ever saw him.

Dan Inosanto

JKD will have to adapt to new training methods and understand the new martial arts that become popular. Training methods are better so the standards should be generally going up.

Cass Magda

At that time I was not that educated so it was hard for me to differentiate things from a technical point of view. What really impressed me was Bruce's speed and power when delivering techniques and his ability to hit us at will.

Pete Jacobs

Teachers shouldn't think that the teaching is a substitute for their own training.

Taky Kimura

I enrolled in UCLA and earned my degree in electrical engineering. I began looking at different martial arts and in 1956 I continued my training under Ed Parker in kenpo karate.

Dan Lee

When Bruce passed away, I decided to privately train and develop what he taught me. I have always taught actively, but only on a private basis.

Ted Wong

Bruce took the principles of wing chun and used them in long range; he could move your weapons out of the way without even making contact in trapping range.

Jerry Poteet

Training at Dan's backyard was very contact oriented. Sparring was the testing ground for every technique.

Ted Lucaylucay

If you don't have sensitivity to "feel" the right moment for applying a given technique or to flow into the next one, it doesn't matter how many locks or chokes you may know.

Larry Hartsell

Bruce had analyzed some fighting systems that nobody was aware of at the time he passed away. If he were still with us, of course, the whole JKD movement would be very different.

Richard Bustillo

Bruce was amazingly fantastic! He was the closest thing to a magician I've ever seen. He had moves that made you realize you were not dealing with a normal person.

Bob Bremer

Dan Inosanto is, in my opinion, a perpetual student. He loves learning new things. He's investigated training methods used in different martial art systems, and some of those training methods were incorporated into his own JKD and shared with his students.

Chris Kent

Bruce Lee developed a method that was brilliantly simple yet highly tactical. Blending the principles of fencing with empty hand martial arts was sheer genius. You may think differently, but I believe if someone is using the term JKD as their personal expression, then their approach should be based upon street specific self-defense fighting that encompasses all of the ranges and draws heavily from the principles of Jun Fan JKD.

Burt Richardson

If you look at Taky Kimura and myself, you would not think that we were taught by the same man.

Ted Wong

There is something very wrong with people claiming to teach "blends of jeet kune do and something else."

John Steven Soet

Tie up with Inosanto and see how well your traps work. Grappling, you say? I've got news, my friend. Any one of the Gracie Brothers will give you a very serious reality check.

Paul Vunak

Although I had some experience in the arts, I was still locked into what Bruce called "the classical mess."

Joe Hyams

Hawkins Cheung told me that Bruce and he had a motto, "One *pak da* to strike down everyone under heaven!" Jeet kune do was his expression of the combat applications, with variations and changes, of the wing chun *pak da* (slapping strike).

Robert Chu

Bruce was able to punch from half an inch away and grind anybody through the wall because he had such complete torque, such a dynamic turning axis and such an explosive pinpointing of energy.

Stirling Silliphant

I had one sparring session with Bruce out in his backyard. He was very mobile and emphasized quite a bit on footwork. He'd stand still and then he would bounce in, skip in real quick, or dart in and out, and left and right.

Leo T. Fong

You have to discover truth for yourself in order to truly understand it. A person can no more give you the truth than they can eat your food for you. You've got to do it yourself.

Chris Kent

The thing that was amazing about Bruce was that he could beat you with his brain.

Dan Inosanto

I realized that Bruce liked to have students with some previous training so they could appreciate more deeply what he was trying to teach.

Dan Lee

I don't think he really liked to go to the ground, but he knew how to dissolve a grappling situation with fingers to the eyes, attacks to the throat and ears, et cetera.

Bob Bremer

Bruce wasn't Superman, but he did things that nobody was capable of doing at that time. Ed Parker was very good himself and I think it is ridiculous to judge him and Bruce against each other. They were doing things differently.

Pete Jacobs

Bruce always taught us to train with the idea of ending a real confrontation as quickly as possible by defeating the opponent in the minimum amount of time.

Taky Kimura

I'm sure Bruce would have evolved and added some good things. Maybe grappling is the only aspect that wasn't stressed much then.

Tim Tackett

Bruce's emphasis was always on efficiency, immediacy and above all, simplicity. His art was indeed "The direct expression of one's feelings with the minimum of movements and energy."

Ted Wong

Training with Bruce was a very revealing experience because he made you aware of your own capabilities. He'd help you to discover your strengths and weaknesses.

Richard Bustillo

Bruce felt that the front leg and hand should be cultivated to be the power weapons, since they were closest to the tar- get. It takes a great deal of skill to hit and kick with the front hand and leg and deliver the same power as other arts do with the rear weapons.

Jerry Poteet

The JKD student today has to be familiar and exposed to all these new methods and approaches like MMA. That's what he may possibly be up against, so if he doesn't understand it then he will be in trouble. You've got to be aware so you can adapt.

Cass Magda

The focal point in the training was contact sparring and you could see all the novices being whacked by the old guys. The old guys were complaining that there weren't decent sparring partners at the academy and most of the young guys quit because they couldn't tolerate the full-blast sparring.

Ted Lucaylucay

Shoot wrestling is a very efficient combination of Russian sambo, judo, Thai boxing, kyokushinkai karate, boxing and wrestling. Carl Gotch incorporated a lot of submission elements together and Satoru Sayama began spreading the art in Japan.

Larry Hartsell

Understanding that we have only a limited number of "tools" on our bodies that can be used to inflict damage on an opponent, isolation training allows full development of those tools.

Paul Vunak

In JKD we want simplicity. But in high-level fighting against a skillful opponent, we must employ a level of complexity that can overcome the high-level defense of the opponent. While maintaining simplicity, Bruce Lee added higher levels of complexity in order to have tools, approaches, and tactics that foiled the defenses of skillful opponents.

Burt Richardson

There is nothing wrong with Dan Inosanto's path. Jeet kune do was simply a boat to get him to a certain destination. There is also nothing wrong with people like Ted Wong or Jerry Poteet preferring to adhere to the original teachings of Bruce Lee.

John Steven Soet

Jeet kuen is a way of meeting, capturing, and controlling your opponent's centerline and center of gravity in the most simple, direct, and economical way.

Robert Chu

From the roundhouse kick, Bruce moved me into more complex combinations. But he would never let me do combinations until he felt that I'd not only mastered individual kicks, but that I was able to relate them to an opponent as part of an intuitive arsenal.

Stirling Silliphant

I hadn't enough background in wing chun, for example, to fully grasp the underlying principles of centerline and 'sticky hands,' so all I could do was imitate the master.

Joe Hyams

According to Dan, when Bruce touched hands with you it was all over because he could totally control you by feeling and re-directing your energy.

Chris Kent

I began to travel to Oakland, where he lived with James Lee, for training updates. He moved to Los Angeles over a year later.

Dan Inosanto

Some of the first-generation guys come down and coach at my school once in a while. I enjoy that and am tremendously grateful and honored.

Cass Magda

I was the number four student to sign up at the Chinatown school. It's not that I have a lot of clear memories about every single class we had there.

Pete Jacobs

Those interested in the arts should accept the fact that there are no short-cuts—there aren't any. Hard work is the main thing and there is no substitute.

Taky Kimura

In the beginning the training with Bruce was very rugged. He was selecting the students so he could make the training very physical.

Dan Lee

You can't learn your "self-expression" through Jeet Kune Do without having a teacher who knows how to guide you from A to Z. You need the core understanding of how the philosophy works and how it affects the physical art.

Tim Tackett

I should stress the importance of the lead hand/foot weapon, that is, the lead punch/kick is the backbone of jeet kune do. To understand the art of JKD, one must completely understand this concept.

Ted Wong

The principles of Jeet Kune Do are; simplicity, economy of motion, longest weapon to the nearest target, to name three. Simple, meaning uncomplicated, not easy!

Jerry Poteet

I've been criticized for what I'm going to say, but I think we were afraid that if we were beaten, the JKD illusion of invincibility would have been destroyed.

Ted Lucaylucay

Find a good boxing gym to polish your hands and a good grappling foundation would be the Brazilian jiu-jitsu system, shoot wrestling, or any solid submission system.

Larry Hartsell

Bruce was real good at subtle fakes, like a boxer. I studied him as much as I could, because he didn't telegraph. He would tell you he was going to hit you in the head, and he'd make a little preliminary movement and boom, he's in there.

Leo T. Fong

Dan Inosanto and I opened the old Kali Academy in Torrance, where we did a great deal of research on the Filipino martial arts.

Richard Bustillo

Bruce was consumed with what he did, and it was no wonder he got so good.

Bob Bremer

We certainly need a small collection of tools that are honed to a very sharp edge. That is essential and it comes naturally out of sparring. You will find something that works well for you, your mindset, and your physical attributes, so you will naturally use it over and over again.

Burt Richardson

What the public has to know is that many of the so called JKD instructors, particularly those who till themselves as "next generation," are not familiar with the core teachings of Bruce Lee. The scope of jeet kune do concepts is very broad. If asked what Bruce Lee would have done to people claiming to teach JKD under this broad definition, the answer would be he'd probably kick their butts.

John Steven Soet

Make sure you don't just go through the motions. Inject full intensity and use the full range of emotional volume. Use your imagination and picture a real opponent in front of you on the heavy bag.

Paul Vunak

Bruce liked the side thrust kick using the whole hip and body. He also made me practice the roundhouse, using the instep or ball of the foot as the striking point into a target, like the upper biceps or the shoulder.

Stirling Silliphant

By the time he left for Hong Kong I could imitate his movements but not execute them with speed and confidence.

Joe Hyams

How do you reconcile Bruce's belief of not giving out belts as an indicator of progress if you're giving them out. Keep in mind that initially Bruce established a form of ranking for his art, but then tossed it out.

Chris Kent

Bruce's approach to martial arts training was very contact oriented. Physical conditioning was a mandatory requirement and he emphasized it.

Dan Inosanto

Change does not mean evolution; it just means you are doing it differently. Change with evolution means that your change has resulted in something being more functional.

Cass Magda

I'm sure Bruce thought we were in very bad shape when compared to him so he wanted to be sure that we could deal with the physical demands of the training.

Pete Jacobs

I am a private person. I like to stay in the woodwork, and I don't think I have that much to offer because my knowledge is limited; but I feel secure with what Bruce taught me.

Taky Kimura

When I started to train under Bruce, I had to get rid of all my preconditioned physical responses, because what I'd learned was just a fixed routine.

Dan Lee

Without roots, people get confused and end up without a structure to grow from. No criteria and no guidelines equals no learning. You can't learn everything at the same time. You need a strong core of something to develop from.

Tim Tackett

In many classical martial arts systems, the foot always precedes the hand in delivering a punch. In Bruce's JKD, it is the reverse. The hand always precedes the foot, and the punch explodes with the whole body weight behind it.

Ted Wong

It's not how much, but how well that matters." You see, Jeet Kune Do is an art of skill. Unlike classical martial arts, it has very little to do with how many techniques or kata you accumulate.

Jerry Poteet

The individual is the important element in the art so it's up to him to apply the JKD principles in order to create a personal style.

Ted Lucaylucay

In my opinion, Lee used fencing terms to try to gain acceptance into the American market. Modern fencing terminology of the "stop hit" is universal—it means to "*jeet*" (intercept), as in wing chun terminology. Many martial arts styles and systems have a "stop hit," Lee was not unique in discovering that intercepting is one of the quickest counters.

Robert Chu

Muay Thai or Savate are very good kickboxing systems. Muay Thai teaches you also how to efficiently use your elbows and knees.

Larry Hartsell

The curriculum base is the same that Bruce had, but we have evolved certain aspects—so we've added and expanded. The basic idea of JKD is to change and evolve.

Richard Bustill

The core JKD structure will give you a framework from which to study other arts and to fill whatever blanks you might have.

Bob Bremer

Today, I use the phrase "pressure testing". Beyond particular techniques or tactics, it is the training methods, that include pressure testing, that are most important in developing a formidable fighter. And that is what JKD is about.

Burt Richardson

A key aspect consistently overlooked is the ability and savvy to get into the deadly trapping/grappling range.

Paul Vunak

Matters became much worse in the 1980's with the growth of the seminar concept, where people would become 'apprentices' and turn around and start teaching what they called JKD the minute Dan's back was turned. In the meantime, people like Chris Kent, Jerry Poteet and Ted Wong were silently observing a covenant not to prostitute Bruce's name or JKD instructors. Only after years of sitting by and watching did these men and their students "go public."

John Steven Soet

One of the things that helped me in the transition was the fact that, through fencing, my reflexes had been tuned to accommodate blindingly fast counter- attacks. I never had been aggressive as a fencer. I seldom initiated an attack. I suppose this springs straight out of my own psyche.

Stirling Silliphant

It seemed to me Bruce's kicks were basically tae kwon do; his hands were unquestionably wing chun and his stance and aggressive posture was that of a boxer.

Joe Hyams

JKD training was totally different to any other style I practiced before. Everything we did in JKD was reality-based.

Chris Kent

I use the JKD approach to training and technical investigation when I work with other arts like kali. You can find some JKD principles in different martial arts.

Dan Inosanto

I felt like Inosanto's intense battery was charging me. He had all these ideas of "systems" he was trying out—sometimes on me! He stressed the conceptual, and interconnections between things.

Cass Magda

JKD is about skill, not technique. And in order to achieve that you need to spar with different people, otherwise you'll always fool yourself into thinking that you can do it.

Pete Jacobs

Bruce's technical nucleus in Seattle was definitely the wing chun system, but he taught us a modified version of it.

Taky Kimura

Sharpen your tools and develop quality speed, accuracy, and power. I recommend practicing realistic fighting in order to develop poise and experience. I think this is the very core of the Jeet Kune Do training.

Dan Lee

For the first day, Dan told me to bring 16-ounce gloves. So I'm standing there with 16-ounce gloves and these guys with 12 and 14-ounce gloves. The first night I had to spar with Bob Bremer and Danny Lee. That alone could make you want not to come back!

Tim Tackett

Bruce studied different systems, but only in order to know what they were doing and how he would deal with those—not necessarily to add more techniques to JKD.

Ted Wong

I saw Bruce use the wing chun dummy, and the way he was hit-ting it and moving it around it sounded like someone was firing a machine gun.

Jerry Poteet

Bruce taught me to dissect time into infinite degrees. It's what he called "playing between the keys" of the piano. It's the understanding that you actually have worlds of time within split seconds to do something else unanticipated while your opponent is committed to his already announced action.

Stirling Silliphant

Another misperception is that if you're not training in the same exact art that Dan is training in at the moment, then you're not doing JKD, or that you've fallen behind and need to be "updated."

Chris Kent

Strictly from a technical point of view I use the method that was taught at Dan's backyard and the Kali Academy, bring it to the gym, glove up and spar. I would test the essentials to find out the truth and do away with all that make believe stuff. That's how I was taught and that's the real JKD.

Ted Lucaylucay

Bruce was very light on his feet, and his footwork was amazing—very deceptive and evasive. He liked to try new things when sparring, but when he really got serious, he'd stop-kick, trap and finish.

Larry Hartsell

A good instructor will always help students find their own way and help them discover the methods that fit their natural ability.

Richard Bustillo

Chinatown school training was very physical and very demanding. Conditioning exercises, punching, and kicking on focus gloves, heavy bag, et cetera. We used to do lots of sensitivity drills from wing chun to improve our trapping skills as well.

Bob Bremer

Simple attacks work great on fighters you outclass. A level of practical complexity is necessary for the higher-level opponents.

Burt Richardson

Every strike or technique, to be effective, must be used at the correct time and range. Many of the trapping and grappling arts need to be in close to apply their special brand of expertise. This is fact.

Paul Vunak

Bruce's methods changed with every lesson he taught. Never did I feel that I was going through some pre-established syllabus, some textbook course of various rote techniques, whereby I had to proceed from page one to page thirty and learn all the successive movements.

Stirling Silliphant

Jun Fan Gung-Fu was the art that formed the basis of Jeet Kune Do.

Ted Lucaylucay

During three years of sparring with him, I never touched him once, even when we were nose to nose. His anticipation of movement and reflexes was just too good.

Joe Hyams

In Dan's backyard, we did a lot of the physical conditioning and tool training on equipment like focus gloves, kicking shields, heavy bags, and top-and-bottom bags. We also did a lot of freelance sparring.

Chris Kent

A JKD practitioner or exponent might be able to perform the JKD techniques efficiently, but a JKD instructor needs a good technical level, and a high level of understanding of JKD philosophy and how these philosophical principles apply to the physical techniques.

Dan Inosanto

To be able to discern what is functional requires understanding the principle in practical application coupled with experience.

Cass Magda

Bruce always wanted to keep the movements simple and, above all, natural—but maintain the principles of physics in order to deliver the punch or the kick with power and speed.

Pete Jacobs

I like the arts where you can test your skills through competition like boxing and kickboxing.

Richard Bustillo

Bruce was familiar with many other Chinese kung-fu styles such as praying mantis, choy lee fut, hung gar, et cetera, but I think he really identified himself with the wing chun method.

Taky Kimura

Bruce always said not to get an accumulation of techniques but to stress the essence of the important ones and make them your own. Sharpen your tools so they become masterpieces.

Dan Lee

The classes in Dan's backyard were two hours every Tuesday and Thursday, and we only practiced Escrima during the last half-hour.

Tim Tackett

I think Lee was more interested in his own development than with the development of a system. He already had his foundation in wing chun and didn't need to spend time giving it to others. Instead, he gave them shortcuts and glimpses of what he was personally working on.

Robert Chu

Bruce didn't go from a wing chun punch to a Western boxing punch. He used certain boxing principles and applied them to wing chun punching in order to make it more effective.

Ted Wong

For the first three months, I was not allowed to use the rear hand. He emphasized hitting with the vertical fist from the right lead. He saw me punching with the rear hand once, and came over and said, "Very good Jerry, but not now— in time."

Jerry Poteet

The minute I began sparring with Bruce I knew that something was wrong. He was moving in and out, I couldn't touch him, and he was tapping me every time he wanted to without me being able to adjust.

Larry Hartsell

When I began training under Bruce it was like going from high school to college. He wanted us to realistically use everything he was teaching.

Bob Bremer

He used the scientific method by taking his techniques into the lab of hard sparring against martial artists of various styles to find out what worked and didn't work.

Burt Richardson

Most people just don't realize how truly intense and fast a real streetfight is. It certainly doesn't help if you've never been in one.

Paul Vunak

Bruce believed in making you achieve your maximum potential as quickly as possible, and in making you believe in the impossible.

Stirling Silliphant

Remember, "Knowing is not enough; you must apply." You've got to take the material you're studying out on the floor and field-test it. You need to see how it works in realistic situations and under pressure.

Chris Kent

We used to skip rope, work on the heavy bag and the air shields, use the focus mitts for many different combinations, practice sensitivity drills and *chi sao*, and do a lot of sparring.

Dan Inosanto

As a direct student you learn a lot of things that aren't usually taught—like tips on making your strategy or technique work better, or a story or anecdote about Bruce Lee. This is what is so valuable to me because it's so personal.

Cass Magda

Bruce paid a lot of attention to each and every one of the students, giving personal tips here and there.

Pete Jacobs

I'm not here to teach people how to fight. If what I'm sharing can help them to feel good about themselves, then I'm happy.

Taky Kimura

Bruce used to experiment with different techniques over-and- over before he would decide whether they were effective or not.

Dan Lee

You don't add something you don't need or something that goes against the basic principles of the art. You need the roots, period.

Tim Tackett

He concentrated on developing speed, reaction time, and methods of delivery, on building power and stamina, and on staying physically fit. This was what Bruce meant by the totality of combat.

Ted Wong

One of Bruce's teachings that I constantly hear is, "Add what is specifically your own." What Bruce meant is to add your own attitude, desire, intention, and mental and psychological approach to training. He did not mean just go ahead and do anything related to martial arts and call it your own personal JKD.

Jerry Poteet

When I began teaching, I realized that I had to emphasize a more classical approach to the training. By that I mean requiring a lot of repetition of techniques.

Ted Lucaylucay

You can't always dictate your own environment to fight, so I believe the best way to prepare yourself for that is to study different arts in order to become well-rounded.

Larry Hartsell

We begin with Bruce's base system, and the physical techniques he was teaching. But after years of training, and when a certain level of understanding is reached, the student reaches their own JKD expression.

Richard Bustillo

Bruce maintained a certain amount of trapping, but you'll notice that when he does trapping it doesn't look like classical Wing Chun. So that's why he went in from the on-guard position, which is a boxers stance.

Leo T. Fong

Bruce never liked the word "style" because he thought the term was very limiting. He realized, though, that the art should be structured in order to teach it to a student in a progressive manner.

Ted Wong

By truly understanding the JKD core, you're more capable of adding certain things in the right way.

Bob Bremer

In JKD, the straight blast has been modified to enable the practitioner to hit with a different flavor and angle, but the repeated piston-like action remains the same and is considered the essence of the technique.

Cass Magda

Failing to understand how the various elements in Jun Fan are bound up into a single "Whole" makes it impossible to master the methods of its practical structuring and planting. It then dissolves into a haphazard accumulation of various pieces of a puzzle without any idea as to what the finished picture will look like.

Tim Tackett

Many of the elements that he believed were functional actually were not. If you don't believe me, you may want to believe what Bruce Lee wrote in a letter to his Wing Chun classmate and oftentimes instructor Wong Shun Leung. "Since I started to practice realistically in 1966 (body protectors, gloves, etc.), I feel that I had many prejudices before, but they were wrong. So, I changed the name of the gist of my study to Jeet Kune Do."

Burt Richardson

When evaluating which style of grappling is the most effective, one must take into consideration that each style has its own strategy and approach to combat.

Paul Vunak

Bruce said, "Let's see what you can do." He took a cushion off the couch and told me to kick it. I did, in the way I thought it should be kicked, which was pitiful—the way a woman would kick a mouse or something. It was probably the worst kick Bruce had ever seen.

Stirling Silliphant

The wing chun that I know is the modified version Bruce taught me and I guess its structure takes away a lot of the impractical things that you can learn in other systems.

Taky Kimura

You need three basic elements: cardiovascular endurance, strength, and flexibility. These are your basics. You should run, work with weights, and stretch.

Ted Wong

Bruce hated big classes. It was a thing where he felt to maintain the quality it had to be one-on-one. And he was right. It's just like a boxing trainer.

Dan Inosanto

The only way we can really interpret or relate to what we are reading is through experience. Somebody who doesn't have any martial arts experience is going to have a definite disadvantage in being able to understand, interpret, and evaluate Bruce's notes as compared to someone who does have experience.

Chris Kent

If you look at Ted Wong, Dan Lee, Bob Bremer, etc... you'll see they have the structure. For instance, if you watch any of them performing what is called "closing the gap," they all perform it the same way, yet they all look a little different doing it.

Cass Magda

Each one of us needed different corrections according to the way we were doing the technique. Bruce would break the movement down and find the best way for each one of us to deliver the technique properly.

Pete Jacobs

Bruce used to tell us that our punches and kicks were our "tools of the trade," so much of the time was spent fine-tuning those.

Dan Lee

Adding for the sake of adding is not a JKD attitude because you may be adding because you lack deep understanding of a JKD technique.

Tim Tackett

According to Bruce Lee, mobility is one of the most neglected attributes of martial arts training. The essence of combat is the art of mobility – to seek our target, while at the same time, avoid being one. In JKD, footwork should be easy, relaxed, and alive.

Ted Wong

There are all these different interpretations of JKD. Some are unrecognizable to me.

Cass Magda

I don't practice jiu-jitsu and call it JKD. It is not fair to the jiu-jitsu people to take their stuff and call it something else—that's not an honorable thing to do.

Tim Tackett

Bruce made fighting exciting and entertaining to learn. He made it what I always felt it should be—a beautiful game of physical and psychological chess, a constant test of oneself.

Stirling Silliphant

Sometimes people can't differentiate between training methods Dan might be using, and an entire art itself; I think this has led to confusion and misunderstanding.

Chris Kent

How can you expect any technique to work unless you repeat it thousands of times and drill it constantly? Some people couldn't deal with the reality of training.

Ted Lucaylucay

Before his death he had over 33 grappling movements in his Jeet Kune Do.

Larry Hartsell

Personal evolution may take you to very different destinations. Some of them are very far from the basic principles of JKD. Not everybody's expression is Jeet Kune Do.

Richard Bustillo

He developed JKD according to his own physical capabilities. He had it figured out for himself.

Bob Bremer

Training for self-defense in the same manner that a boxer, fencer, or MMA athlete prepares for a fight is what makes JKD so functional. It illustrates how Bruce Lee was so far ahead of his time. Dry land swimming just can't prepare you for the realities of the ocean.

Burt Richardson

The longer, and more intensity one trains in different arenas (i.e. boxers, wrestlers, savate men, Thai boxers, etc.), the more equipped one is like absorb what is useful, reject what is useless, and add what is specifically one's own.

Paul Vunak

I found Bruce's training methods fascinating. They were not structured. They were always free, very spontaneous and improvisational.

Stirling Silliphant

I think that the most important attribute or quality for any JKD practitioner to possess is adaptability; the ability to fit in with any type of opponent.

Chris Kent

For a wing chun man, *chi sao* is probably the most important aspect in training and it dictates the students' approach to fighting.

Taky Kimura

Bruce was very intuitive and instinctive as far as teaching goes, perhaps because dealing with a one-on-one situation is very different from teaching 30 people at the same time.

Dan Inosanto

The original package of techniques has to be limited, if it is going to stay true to its design. Everyone who teaches needs to learn the core principles and techniques of Bruce Lee's Jeet Kune Do.

Cass Magda

Many instructors wrongly present a mishmash of martial arts techniques and call it "Jeet Kune Do."

Tim Tackett

Bruce always talked about "emotional content." Well, in order to have that emotional content you need to understand yourself. And this is paramount if you want to go beyond that physical level.

Pete Jacobs

The fighting distance in JKD is defined as "the continually shifting relationship, depending on the speed, agility, and control of both fighters. It is a constant, rapid shifting of ground, seeking the slightest closing which will greatly increase the chances of hitting the opponent."

Ted Wong

Since Bruce's death, Dan has been the preeminent and foremost spokesperson for JKD, teaching and educating people around the world about the art and philosophy.

Chris Kent

In Los Angeles, Bruce began to emphasize wing chun less and less in his teaching. I guess his evolution took him to the point where he perceived certain limitations in *chi sao*.

Ted Wong

Bruce knew the yin/yang principles. Definitely, this Chinese concept has been influential in Jeet Kune Do. Bruce saw his JKD principles in terms of the Taoist philosophy of yin and yang.

Dan Lee

Bruce wanted me to develop the front weapons to perfection, since they're going to be doing most of the work. He didn't want me to feel the power in the rear hand until I had properly developed the front.

Jerry Poteet

I saw the original teachers of JKD being exploited and I knew in time that they would be pushed aside because others would take their knowledge and claim it as their own.

Ted Lucaylucay

Because of my size and background in judo and wrestling I've always felt very comfortable in grappling.

Larry Hartsell

"Jun Fan" was Bruce's Chinese name and that's the name he gave to the gung fu he put together. Jeet Kune Do was his personal art, philosophy and expression.

Richard Bustillo

We did a lot of sparring. All the training was contact oriented. We trained pretty much like boxers.

Bob Bremer

Jeet Kune Do is a fighting art, so every instructor must be able to fight. That's why the physical test is predominantly moderate intensity sparring. No sparring, no JKD. Pretty simple.

Burt Richardson

A JKD man strives to divorce the word "theory" from his arsenal. This, again, is done by implementing good old-fashioned fight-time.

Paul Vunak

The first thing Bruce did with me was to concentrate on my body movement and particularly on what he called "closing the gap," the relationship between you and your opponent.

Stirling Silliphant

JKD is about taking every single tool that you have and developing a total understanding of its strengths and weaknesses, and how and when to use it against any type of opponent.

Chris Kent

Some of the basic techniques now were big secrets in the mid-60s. I never asked him why, because he was the sifu. If he didn't want me to teach certain Jeet Kune Do material, I didn't. I kept things the way he wanted.

Dan Inosanto

Now the whole nature of what JKD was has changed into something else. It no longer follows its design—its principles. We have to be wary of not burdening our JKD with a lot of unrelated techniques.

Cass Magda

The use of the rear heel up was something very natural for him. He found this to be "true" for him and then he read a book and found that a great fencer named Aldo Nadi was doing the same thing.

Pete Jacobs

Bruce probably realized the limitations of certain aspects of wing chun when trying to practice "sticky hands" with someone like Kareem Abdul Jabbar.

Taky Kimura

Bruce stressed the principles of pliability in order to flow the opponent's energy and then counter it, like water flowing and fitting into any space. He taught us that our technique should be the result of our opponent's technique.

Dan Lee

A JKD practitioner cannot study ten times as hard or ten times as long as a martial artist who specializes in one method. He must train ten times as smart. The ultimate goal is to get as good as your genetic potential will allow in each of the elements – and to shift from one to another without stopping the mind to think about it.

Tim Tackett

To control the distance, one has to utilize good mobility and good footwork through quick shuffles, short shuffles, quick advance, short advance, quick lunges and changes in direct split second.

Ted Wong

In JKD most of the offense is done with the lead leg and hand.

Jerry Poteet

I feel that the JKD philosophy of liberation has become a prison for many JKD practitioners. I've seen people blindly following the stereotype of Jeet Kune Do.

Ted Lucaylucay

Bruce taught me to find what worked for me and that's what I keep doing. I'm an in-fighter and what works for me may not work for someone else because of differences in size, mental attitude, strength, et cetera.

Larry Hartsell

Not only has the art evolved and new avenues opened to research and investigate new methods, but the attitude and mentality of the practitioners has changed as well.

Richard Bustillo

Bruce went on to talk about the body being the key. Look at his writings and notes: "Find the cause of your ignorance," "You are it," "Don't go looking for secret moves," "The answer is with you," "In this way you become your own teacher."

Chris Kent

For Bruce, being in top physical condition was a mandatory requirement.

Bob Bremer

When we started on hand movements, he introduced me to some of the historic background on the use of hands, wrists and arms.

Stirling Silliphant

The beauty of taking this road is that it truly builds character. People often talk about martial arts as a character-building activity. You don't build character when everything's going great. You build character through overcoming difficulties. This is another reason why Bruce Lee said that JKD is not for everyone. You have to fail, engage in serious self-reflection, then have the courage to go back and repeat the process over and over again until failure is minimized.

Burt Richardson

People proficient in the very lethal range of trapping, where one must enter into close range, find that the most efficient way to enter into this range is with PIA.

Paul Vunak

Jun Fan Gung Fu was the system Bruce had before developing Jeet Kune Do. It was the base system he taught in Seattle and Oakland.

Dan Inosanto

When you look at JKD you see the wing chun influence, the theory and trapping, but you don't see the body postures, footwork, and movement style of wing chun. You see the boxing element but not the stance and stylized movement of a boxer.

Cass Magda

Wing Chun is a great system and a very good fighting method. Definitely, if you study this style, you can see a lot of similarities—but mainly in the conceptual part of the art.

Pete Jacobs

Bruce called me one day and said that *chi sao* was not the focal point anymore, as we had thought earlier. I was shocked.

Taky Kimura

When you are fighting there is no such thing as prearranged action. One has to wait quietly and patiently and move harmoniously with the attack that is coming toward you.

Dan Lee

Jun fan is the foundation from which jeet kune do eventually evolved. It is what Bruce Lee taught and referred to as his "martial way" before the term jeet kune do came into existence. If JKD is a way of thinking, training, researching, and experimenting, the jun fan martial arts are a primary vehicle to get you there.

Tim Tackett

I was training at the *kwoon* in Chinatown and one day he was watching and said to somebody, "I'm gonna take him as a private student." And that was it.

Ted Wong

A lot of JKD people have thrown a lot of stuff out the window because they read that Bruce Lee said so. What a big mistake.

Ted Lucaylucay

He had analyzed some fighting systems that nobody was aware of at the time he passed away. If he were still with us, of course, the whole JKD movement would be very different.

Richard Bustillo

When I began training under Bruce it was like going from high school to college. He wanted us to realistically use everything he was teaching.

Bob Bremer

Bruce Lee's belief was that one could go directly to Chi Sao and, after a reasonable amount of time practicing, segue into trapping while sparring.

Paul Vunak

When Bruce started teaching me kicking, he started with a simple, straightforward front kick, off both the right and left legs. In Bruce's case, this kick was totally different from all the others.

Stirling Silliphant

In the beginning, Dan just kind of let us duke it out with each other. I have to tell you that I had my clock cleaned numerous times by people like Richard Bustillo, Daniel Lee, and Bob Bremer.

Chris Kent

I still teach the original program of Bruce Lee that I like to call "Jun Fan Gung Fu" or "The Gung Fu Method of Jun Fan. This system comes from him but I also provide the students with the philosophy of Jeet Kune Do so they can experience, research, and train—thus exploring as many styles as they want.

Dan Inosanto

Bruce developed a very personal approach, and the final product or physical technique became really different from the original Wing Chun system.

Pete Jacobs

Bruce paced himself as a teacher according to my capabilities as student.

Taky Kimura

JKD is a journey of self-knowledge to the ultimate reality in combat. JKD is not daily increase but daily decrease— hacking away the unessential.

Dan Lee

Each of the aspects of the Jun Fan martial arts, while being a separate entity, is also part of the "whole" and most be able to be linked with all of the other aspects.

Tim Tackett

Why is a wing chun trapping combination a "liberated" technique and a kenpo self-defense technique is a "classical mess?" There is no difference between the two.

Ted Lucaylucay

"Jun Fan" was Bruce's Chinese name and that's the name he gave to the gung fu he put together. Jeet Kune Do was his personal art, philosophy and expression.

Richard Bustillo

The first time I went to Bruce's house in Culver City, and these guys were there, the entire practice session was devoted to timing.

Stirling Silliphant

Bruce was using a very different structure than the rest of the styles. We were using Western boxing, wing chun trapping, wrestling, and things like that. None of those aspects could be used in kenpo.

Larry Hartsell

Bruce studied the body motion and the physical signs that developed before any action actually began. He could notice these small clues and react to them—thereby intercepting your motion.

Bob Bremer

While JKD does have principles that one may interpret as rules or precursors (i.e. maintain centerline, learning to fight at all four ranges, etc.) none of the aforementioned characteristics detract from one's individualism.

Paul Vunak

I was trying to be very dedicated to what he was teaching. On other hand, I was speaking Cantonese to him. I was coming from the same place so maybe he could relate a little bit more to me.

Ted Wong

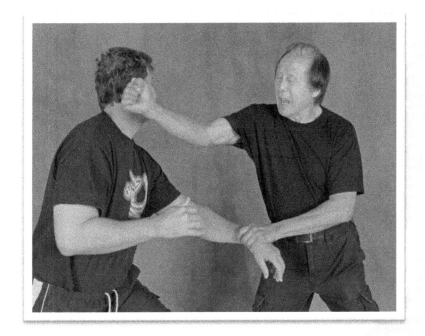

At Dan's backyard, we worked a lot of trapping hands and did a lot of energy training exercises. We did a bit of grappling, mostly locks and chokes and a few takedowns.

Chris Kent

You can put different arts together and the final product will not "be" Jeet Kune Do. bruce never wanted to accumulate unnecessary knowledge. What he added, he did because he was making what he had more efficient.

Dan Inosanto

The main idea behind the straight blast is to blast in when an opening appears and maintain a strong forward pressure on the opponent. This tends to keep the opponent on the defensive for the moment.

Cass Magda

If Bruce wanted to develop mobility, he didn't look at ten different stances and try to get the best from them. What he did was to "feel" the most convenient way of moving and delivering power at the same time. He analyzed the way the human body moves and from that conclusion he researched and developed his stance and footwork.

Pete Jacobs

Probably because of my close relationship with him as a friend, I am the only guy in Seattle that saw the JKD level that he was into whenever he came up here.

Taky Kimura

You don't use fixed techniques as your only techniques because all fixed patterns are incapable of adapting to changing situations. That principle implies constant experimentation and innovation to discover your own potential—to find out what really works best for you individually.

Dan Lee

"Jun Fan" was the term Bruce used to describe his modified version of wing chun that included a few things from other Chinese systems. You can say that Jun Fan was the forerunner of Jeet Kune Do.

Tim Tackett

We begin with Bruce's base system, and the physical techniques he was teaching. But after years of training, and when a certain level of understanding is reached, the student reaches their own JKD expression.

Richard Bustillo

First you heard, "Total freedom in combat," and yet the moment you performed a high kick you heard: "That's flashy, that's not JKD. You won't do that in the street!"

Ted Lucaylucay

While it's true that I don't think that JKD is for everyone, I do think that it has something to offer everybody.

Chris Kent

Bruce always said the leg is the more powerful weapon, but, ultimately, the man who can punch better will be the one who will win. He taught me the "sticky hand" technique from wing chun system, and we did that blindfolded.

Stirling Silliphant

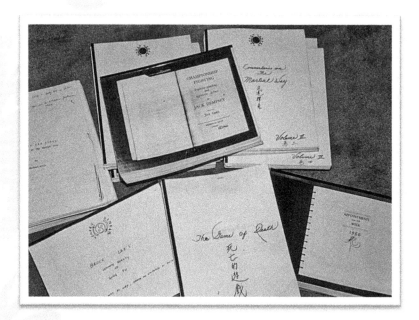

Early in 1966, although the seeds of change had been planted years before, Bruce began to adjust the footwork, the stances, and the angles of the techniques to the point that it was not wing chun anymore.

Dan Inosanto

JKD does have a unique way of explaining it so that it will relate to any style. I think that it shows that these principles aren't exclusive to JKD and can exist in other evolved arts, too.

Cass Magda

There are many different tactics used in Jeet Kune Do, not just intercepting.

Ted Wong

Principles such as simplicity and economy of motion are the foundation of Wing Chun and also of JKD, but the physical technique, the way you move, is different. The essence is there but the physical expression is not the same.

Pete Jacobs

Bruce's straight punch was pretty much the same but the footwork he was using in Los Angeles was from fencing. He realized that he had to be able to punch and hit targets from a longer distance than a classic wing chun man—he wanted to be more mobile as well.

Taky Kimura

JKD is really a mixture of three different elements— Western fencing, Western boxing and wing chun.

Tim Tackett

The curriculum base is the same that Bruce had, but we have evolved certain aspects—so we've added and expanded. The basic idea of JKD is to change and evolve.

Richard Bustillo

Bruce modified the whole structure of his way of fighting. He added several elements from Western boxing, fencing and Northern Shaolin and came up with a whole different system that, at a certain moment in time, he called Jeet Kune Do.

Ted Wong

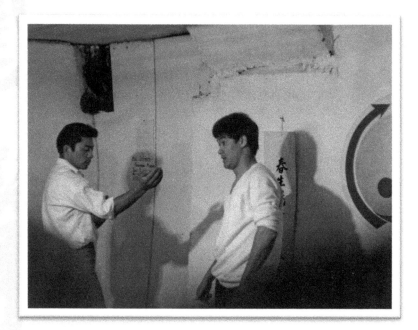

Martial arts training holds up a mirror in which we see ourselves. As you train, you learn about yourself. The problem is that self-discovery is not always a comfortable thing.

Chris Kent

Bruce was a great believer in not being hit. He felt there was no reason ever to be hit unless you failed yourself.

Stirling Silliphant

Whatever Bruce absorbed from a system, it had to fit in to his personal base system. In fact, even if you don't realize it, the criteria for absorbing is based on your conditioning as a practitioner of a particular style.

Dan Inosanto

On seminars Inosanto would relate certain JKD principles and concepts to other arts for a better understanding.

Cass Magda

You can avoid being hit in two ways: either by blocking the attack or by evading it. Bruce preferred the latter. He didn't believe in wasting the energy required to block because he considered blocking a form of attack.

Stirling Silliphant

Bruce found other truths in combat that were not within the boundaries of the wing chun system, so he simply moved on and developed his own thing that he ended up calling Jeet Kune Do.

Pete Jacobs

The main difference between the phases was in the delivery systems of the techniques and the training methods that he developed after being exposed to other arts such as boxing and Western fencing.

Taky Kimura

You can use some of the Jeet Kune Do principles and concepts to analyze and improve other arts that you practice or teach, but that doesn't mean those arts are JKD.

Tim Tackett

JKD has a structure and in order to preserve his art from being diluted it is very important to establish that structure as a base—a foundation for everyone to learn.

Ted Wong

Training with Bruce was a very revealing experience because he made you aware of your own capabilities. He'd help you to discover your strengths and weaknesses.

Richard Bustillo

Bruce looked at the roots of all forms of unarmed combat in their totality, seeing the common denominators that connected the best components of all styles.

Chris Kent

The straight blast in jeet kune do is a devastatingly effective technique. It is the epitome of simplicity; in fact, it is so simple in execution that, at a casual glance, there doesn't seem to be much to it.

Cass Magda

My students don't expect me to do things as Bruce did and this takes a lot of pressure away from me. I try to help the students to find the best way of making the JKD work for them.

Pete Jacobs

Our training emphasized contact sparring with headgear, gloves, and shin guards—that was something very uncommon then.

Taky Kimura

One of the main theories of defense in JKD is that the best form of defense is a good offense. Rather than attempting to block a kick or punch, the idea is to try to intercept it with your own kick or punch.

Tim Tackett

There is a technical structure and foundation developed by Bruce himself—this is the base system. All these techniques exemplify the fundamental concepts and principles of Jeet Kune Do.

Ted Wong

Bruce really tried to hit me, and when he wanted to, he did. However, I could avoid perhaps three out of four ordinary attacks, and eventually I reached the point where elusiveness was—and always will be—one of my strong assets.

Stirling Silliphant

Over the years, I've run across some JKD instructors who were able to perform dozens of techniques from a number of different arts but were unable to put them together into a cohesive "whole" or demonstrate the core tenets of JKD.

Chris Kent

Bruce used to say, "Footwork first, footwork second, and footwork third."

Ted Wong

To "add what is specifically your own" doesn't mean to add anything for the sake of being different or to make yourself or style unique and different from everyone else.

Cass Magda

The principles of simplicity, directness, and efficiency were already his guidelines during his time in Seattle.

Taky Kimura

There's nothing wrong with using a training method from savate or Thai boxing to improve certain physical attributes very important in Jeet Kune Do—but it doesn't make savate or Thai boxing "Jeet Kune Do."

Tim Tackett

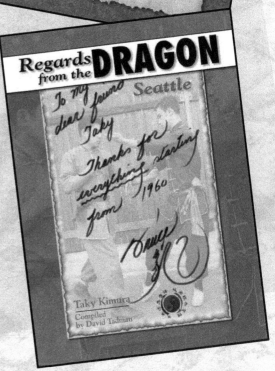

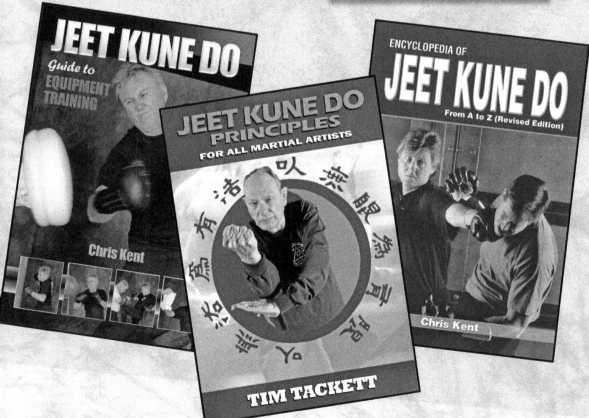

NOTES

Printed in the USA
CPSIA information can be obtained
at www.ICGtesting.com
LVHW071350061024
793038LV00012B/103